# From a Pastor to the Reader-Flock

Dear co-Laborer in Christ,

"How could a good God allow pain and suffering in the world?" is an age-old question that many Christians continue to hear from thoughtful unbelievers as well as disillusioned believers. My friend, John Dozier offers deeply personal and biblically reliable answers for such seekers in his new book.

In a letter written in 1949, C.S. Lewis said, "God, who foresaw your tribulation, has specially armed you to go through it, not without pain but without stain." John Dozier is a living illustration of Lewis' words. Though John has endured the indescribably painful trials of a difficult childhood, the loss of his mother early in life, numerous broken relationships, and the suicide of his father on Christmas night 2002, they have not "stained" him. To describe the same truth in Tim Keller's words, suffering has made John "better not bitter."

Guided by the tender hands of Christ the Great Physician, John performs open heart surgery on himself in front of all of us. In response to his Savior's grace, John reveals his heart for the glory of God and the blessing of his people. Not only is this a timely message, John's writing it down for us is itself an example of the Gospel message of service, "Not for ourselves…" (Romans 15:1; Psalm 115:1).

John urges Christians to live through their present suffering with purpose and without self-pity in order to experience and express the beautiful blessing God is creating.

Many years ago George MacDonald gave the same testimony: "It has been well said that no man ever sank under the burden of the day. It is when tomorrow's burden is added to the burden of today that the weight is more than a man can bear. Never load yourselves so, my friends. If you find yourselves so loaded, at least remember this: it is your own doing, not God's. He begs you to leave the future to Him and mind the present."

This book will be a blessing both for you and for those your life touches.

Sincerely in Christ,
*George Robertson*
Senior Pastor, First Presbyterian Church
Augusta, Georgia

# TAKE HEART

## God Has a Perfect Plan for Your Pain

John O. Dozier, Jr.

Copyright © 2016
John O. Dozier, Jr.

Feast of the Heart, LLC Publishing
FeastoftheHeart.org

All rights reserved. No part of this book may be used or reproduced by any means, graphic, electronic, or mechanical, including photocopying, recording, taping or by any information storage retrieval system without the written permission of the publisher except in the case of brief quotations embodied in critical articles and reviews.

All scripture quotations are "ESV" translations are taken from The Holy Bible: English Standard Version, ©2001, Wheaton: Good News Publishers. Used by permission. All rights reserved.

The opinions expressed by the author are not necessarily those of 40 Day Publishing.

Interior illustrations by Steve Edwards
SteveEdwardsStudio.com

ISBN-13: 978-1539489481
ISBN-10: 1539489485

Certain stock imagery © BigStock Images
Any people depicted in stock imagery provided by BigStock are models, and such images are being used for illustrative purposes only.

Formatting by Daniel Mawhinney
www.40DayPublishing.com

Cover design by Jonna Feavel
www.40DayGraphics.com

Printed in the United States of America

# Dedications

This book is dedicated first and foremost to the awesome Triune God of the universe—Father, Son and Holy Spirit with whom I have had the unmerited gift and unspeakable honor and pleasure of getting to know more and more during the course of my story and spiritual journey. Since before the time I did not know God— when he relentlessly pursued me—to the present time, when I know little else, what can I first acknowledge? "Our God is an awesome God!"

Second, to my wife Peggy and children, Polly and Teddy. Peggy has been amazingly patient with me as I have run up so many mountain tops and tumbled down into so many valleys. Most would have given up on this "'ole runner" long ago. My family has been an anchor and lighthouse. Even as I have been shipwrecked by my own poor compass settings, they have never abandoned ship.

Third, to the legions of angels, saints and messengers God has placed into my life—in the form of myriad colors, creeds and credentials and from places around the world. I have been immeasurably blessed by so many people God's providence has supplied me over the years. There are a handful of particularly stalwart encouragers who, at every turn, have pressed me to push onwards and upwards towards the goal.

Fourth, to my dad and mom—both gone now—who have meant so much to me in great and good ways and, at times, not so great ways. I now see how embracing all of them—in my own great and gruesome heart—I harbor no regrets that cannot be easily swallowed up in God's everlasting arms by his absolute truth and everlasting love. I am what I am, by biological birth and spiritual rebirth, it's all to the glory of God. The spiritual will triumph for all eternity while biological will mark my personal story—mightily redeemed by God.

Finally, to all of my extended family who have been along on so many parts of my amazing journey. What a family they have been! As God continues to ordain our earthly journeys, we grow closer together as the God of the infinite reveals his intimate plan to each of us separate, yet bound together as we travel forth in faith.

As the centerpiece of this book has to do with things so personal and yet so universal, the first circle of family is where the ripples of any declaration from me—dropped into the apparent calm of life—will have an impact. I pray that the disruption be all to God's glory and other's blessing.

Amen.

# Table of Contents

Dedications ..................................................................... 5

Foreword ........................................................................ 13

Preface ........................................................................... 15

    Take Heart .................................................................. 16

    Two Kinds of People .................................................. 18

    Bitter or Better? Only Two Ways to Respond to Life's Unavoidable Pain ......................................................... 19

    A Bird's-Eye Before We Begin .................................. 20

1 The Christmas Crèche and Heartbreaking Crisis .......... 27

    Miraculous Moments ................................................ 28

    Not If, but When ....................................................... 29

    The Christmas Crèche and a Heartbreaking Crisis ..... 30

    The Glory of God's Story: Creation, Fall, Redemption, Consummation ........................................................... 31

    A Take at Our Heart Story ........................................ 36

    A Most Dreadful Change of Heart ............................ 37

    Life in a Horribly Broken World .............................. 38

    Suffering Flipped Upside Down by God—Father, Son, and Holy Spirit ............................................................ 41

2 We Can't Hear God's Protocol for Redemptive Suffering Enough ..................................................................... 43

    The Weeping—Free Falls and Foundations ................ 43

        Application in brief ..................................................... 44

    The Window—More Sinful and More Loved ............ 44

        Application in brief ..................................................... 45

    The Way—Moving Back into the Chaos, Redeemed to Redeem ............................................................................ 45

        Application in brief ..................................................... 46

    Foundations First: Have You Been Born Again? ........ 47

    Or Living Outside Christ ............................................... 47

    Take Pause: Being Sanctified Is Preceded by Being Saved .................................................................................. 50

3 Living in a Culture of Comfort ......................................... 53

    "Theodicy" Is Going Unanswered by the Steward of God's Aim and Answer: The Church ............................ 54

    The Church's Wake-Up Call ......................................... 55

    Don't Get Comfy Here! .................................................. 56

    God Infinitely and Intimately Loves Your Heart ........ 57

    Getting to the Heart of the Matter: It's a Matter of the Heart .................................................................................. 58

4 Take Heart! ............................................................................ 61

    Getting to the Heart of the Heart .................................. 61

    The Heart of the Matter: Good News to Everyone Who Believes .............................................................................. 63

## *TAKE HEART*

Aspirations, Affections, and Exponential Complications ................................................................................... 64

The Heart and Its "Precious" ........................................... 68

Pause. Breathe. Slow (Way) Down: Even if It's Super Hard ................................................................................ 69

Take Hope ........................................................................ 71

Take Heart ........................................................................ 72

5 The Weeping: Free Falls and Foundations ..................... 75

Applying Genesis 1:1, John 1:1, and Deuteronomy 31:6 ........................................................................................... 75

Crisis Happens ................................................................. 78

Family and Story: What's Most Personal Is Most Universal ........................................................................... 78

Out of Nowhere Heartbreak Can Happen .................... 85

The Free Fall and Foundations of Christmas Night ... 89

A Reminder: The Primacy of Free Falls and Foundations ...................................................................... 93

6 The Window: Fallen, Forgiven, Free ............................... 97

Applying Romans 1:18 and Romans 8:1 ....................... 97

All Weeping Opens (Cracks, Pries, Blasts) a Window into Your Heart .............................................................. 101

The Pain and the Blessing of Looking In ................... 102

Hearts in the Fiery Furnace to be Transformed and Set Free .................................................................................. 106

The Paraclete\* and Peering In ..................................... 109

We Have to Spend the Time to Take Care of Our Hearts ...... 112

Don't Waste the Cutting in the Curse of Suffering .. 113

Count the Blessings of Better Knowing Your Heart 114

7 The Way: Bringing Our Transformed Hearts Back into the Chaos .............. 119

Applying Ezekiel 11:19; Romans 8:28, 12:2; and Job 19:25 ...... 119

Order Matters: Foundation First, Window Second .. 122

An Extra Portion of God's Proof, Power, Provision, and Preparation ...... 126

Reentering the Chaos of Life: Take Careful Stock .... 128

Mark the Change of Heart: Less Stone, More Flesh 131

Moan the Purpose of the Spirit: Less Me, More Christ ...... 136

Marvel the Mercy of God: Less Whining, More Worship ...... 140

Move the Mountain with Faith: Less Ruminating, More Redeeming ...... 147

We Have Been Redeemed to Redeem ...... 150

Job: On the Other Side of Suffering ...... 153

God's People Are Called to Move into the Chaos Every Day ...... 157

In Closing Take Close and Careful Stock of Your Heart ...... 159

## TAKE HEART

God's Protocol for Redemptive Suffering: Just for You ............................................................................. 159

A Plea to Know and Remember the Condition of Your Heart before the Next Heartbreak Occurs ................. 161

Your Weeping (Gen. 1:1; John 1:1; Deut. 31:6) ......... 162

Your Window (Rom. 1:18; Rom. 8:1) .......................... 166

Your Way (Ezek. 11:19; Rom. 8:28; 12:2; Job 19:25) 169

1. Mark the Change of Heart: Less Stone, More Flesh 175

2. Moan the Purpose of the Spirit: Less Me, More Christ .............................................................................. 176

3. Marvel the Mercy of God: Less Whining, More Worship ......................................................................... 177

4. Move the Mountain with Faith: Less Ruminating, More Redeeming ............................................................ 177

Mark, Moan, Marvel, Move…This! ............................ 179

Take Heart, Take Hope, but Take Note ...................... 181

Don't Be Surprised, Consider It All Joy: The Cycle of Suffering until Jesus Returns—It Will Make an Eternity of Difference .................................................................. 184

Christian, Get Your "So That" Deep: The God of All Comfort Comforts "So That" ........................................ 188

A Bird's-Eye Before We End ........................................ 188

"The Weeping, the Window, the Way" Bible Chapter-Verse Reference .................................................................. 191

Chapter One: The Christmas Crèche and Heartbreaking Crisis..................................................................191

Chapter Two: We Can't Hear God's Protocol for Redemptive Suffering Enough......................................196

Chapter Three: Living in a Culture of Comfort........200

Chapter Four: Take Heart.............................................201

Chapter Five: The Weeping: Free Falls and Foundations ......................................................................................208

Chapter Six: The Window: Fallen, Forgiven, Free....209

Chapter Seven: The Way: Bringing Our Transformed Hearts Back into the Chaos...........................................213

In Closing: Take Close and Careful Stock of Your Heart ......................................................................................220

God's Redemptive Plan..................................................231

Take Heart! There's a Person, a Promise, and Perfect Plan in Place..................................................................231

Union with Jesus Christ: The Context for all God's Work ..............................................................................240

About the Author............................................................243

About Feast of the Heart, LLC:......................................245

# Foreword

Take Heart is the second project I have worked on with John for the purposes of extending the reach and blessing of his first book, "The Weeping, the Window, the Way: Will Suffering Make You Bitter or Better?"

I'm honored and blessed by this opportunity because I believe John's story is powerful, and more importantly, I believe God's redemptive story is even more powerful still. The miracle that occurred on Christmas night between God, John, and his dying father was profound, high, deep, and, very importantly, "not for himself" (Rom. 15:1).

In reality, the original story and details are much too much to contain in this booklet. But the hope of extending the blessing God has in store for those who turn to Him in their tiny or tumultuous trials is just too great not to try and get it into more hearts, spirits, and lives lived out for Jesus Christ. God weeps about our tears, but He weeps deeper still at wasted tears. Please don't waste yours. I recommend you take heart with all the confidence that God's perfect plan can transform every tear into a triumph.

—Jeremy Bedenbaugh

Jeremy Bedenbaugh earned his M.Div. from Covenant Theological Seminary and currently serves as the Lead Pastor of The Journey, a church in St. Louis, Missouri. Jeremy also helped write and edit "The Weeping, the Window, the Way—IN COMMUNITY," a Community Group Study Guide of John's first book. Online at: http://www.feastoftheheart.org/weeping-window-way/in-the-community

# Preface

Dearest Reader,

This book is a plea, an unabashed entreaty to allow the God of the universe to meet you in your pain, to transform you through your pain. Imagine if it were possible to experience God in times of suffering. What if your suffering could lead to a renewed understanding of your heart, God's heart, and humanity's heart? What if your suffering could change and empower you to face a world of chaos? What if your pain could lead you to find greater eternal purpose in your life? Imagine.

That's what this book is about. And if you're like me—and will admit what we hold most dear in our imagination as being the ideal, in many instances—you're in for a real blessing: God's ideal, his quintessential desire for us, is that he has a perfect plan for our pain—if we will only know and practice it.

This is a book on suffering, a unique look at one of life's deepest realities. Most books like this approach suffering only philosophically or theologically, from an ivory tower, or they approach it unrealistically, as if there are ten easy steps to fixing your life. This book is different. It springs from my own deep suffering and tragedy as well as an in-depth study. It is rooted deeply in the theology of the Bible while also showing clear and practical applications in the midst of pain, big or small. It will allow you to honestly deal with dark realities, and help you see that darkness is not the only reality but is overcome by the Light. This book will challenge you in profound ways, but please understand great change happens only through great challenge.

Boiled down from my original, 384-page book/workbook "The Weeping, The Window, and The Way," this is a "love letter" written to anyone who has experienced suffering, who is presently experiencing suffering, or who will experience suffering of any kind—in other words, it's written to every human being who has, is, or will ever be born.

## Take Heart

The title Take Heart is intentionally used to provide a compassionate promise that, in the midst of your pain, and in Christ, God is powerfully and perfectly at work. As we take this journey together, you're going to find there are many ways to express what Take Heart means. My use of this idiom is as simple yet rich and robust as God intends it.

Positively, Take Heart encompasses ideas and actions like the following:

- "God is with you. Trust him, his promises, he will not abandon you in this time of need."
- "Become confident, courageous, and especially patient during a difficult situation."
- "Have hope by means of consolation, liberation, relief, and/or solace."

## *TAKE HEART*

- "There's help for the hurting. Be brave, and stay connected to God, and his community of faith."
- "Be encouraged, the good will win out."
- "Get outside, raise your gaze, and remember the God who created and sustains all things."
- "Slow down and remember what you are thankful for."
- "You can't rush or uproot ideas that have taken so long to form and put down deep roots in your life."
- "Remember, God has a plan of redemption in place, not simply healing: your suffering can transform you into a wounded healer and a beacon of hope."

Negatively, Take Heart does not include the plethora of surface solutions and bad advice like the following:

- "Buck up—time heals all wounds."
- "It'll pass."
- "Don't question God."
- "No pain, no gain."
- "Keep a stiff upper lip."
- "I know what you're going through."
- "Eat, drink, and be merry."
- "Not to fret…Jesus suffered."
- "Don't worry, be happy."
- "Just try [so-and-so]."
- "The problem is probably [so-and-so]."
- "If I were you, I'd…"
- "I don't know why bad things happen to good people."

Such pithy yet pathetic colloquialisms not only take a far too simplistic, reductionistic approach to offering comfort and assuaging pain, but are motivated by our denial of our own wounds, our inability to simply be present and enter into another's pain, and our unwillingness to stop arguing against another's painful state of heart—because we are arguing against our own.

## Two Kinds of People

The very fabric of our broken world means that the question of experiencing trials in life is not about if but when. The question is not if we will suffer—we absolutely will—but rather what that suffering will produce in and through us. As Pastor Tim Keller said,

*There are only two kinds of people in the world. Both are sufferers. There are the people who build their trust on things beside God so that when suffering comes it takes away the sources of their joy so they become sadder and sadder, and madder and madder, and worse. And then there are the people who suffer, but who seek to build their trust on God, on the basis of his infinite suffering for us on the cross, so that God becomes the source of their joy. When suffering comes in their lives, it drives them into deeper joy. It drives them more into God. And so suffering makes them better and better, and more like Jesus.*

*There are only two kinds of people in the world! They're both going to suffer. There's the kind of person that suffering makes worse, because the source of their joy is being taken away. And there's the kind of person who suffering makes better because the suffering is pushing them towards the one source of joy that is not subject to circumstances. Jesus Christ suffered not so that we might not suffer, but rather when we suffer, we could become more like him! (The Sufferer, sermon by Pastor Tim Keller, Redeemer Presbyterian Church, New York, March 7, 2004)*

You might want to carefully read Keller's words again. It's one of the pithiest, realistic, and most polarizing, truthful, and loving offerings about living in a broken world, along with God's redemptive plan, that there is.

## Bitter or Better? Only Two Ways to Respond to Life's Unavoidable Pain

This book is an expression of my heart's deepest desire for every person that they choose to be made better rather than bitter, that they pause and remember God's heart to push them toward their true source of joy and show them his plan for our pain. Whatever you do, don't bow to internal fear or external pressure to "just get through it" or "get back to normal"—take a breath and ask God for the patience and strength you will need. In God's purview, there is only one "norm" in the realms of what's normal for the suffering Christian: heart, mind, soul and strength conformity more and more to the likeness of Jesus Christ. We cannot do this without the God of the Bible, who descended from infinity, and loves us all the way down to the deepest, most intimate depth of our hearts.

Even now, my trials continue to push me toward "the one source of joy that is not subject to circumstances"—Jesus Christ, his infinite love, and his suffering upon the cross for me—as a conduit, overflow of and for his love and truth to others in my life. This book, the story of how God broke my stony heart to transform it, is not just my story but also the story of God's purposes for every human being. Just as the psalmist who trusted God not just in good times but especially in suffering says,

> **The LORD is my rock, my fortress and my deliverer; my God is my rock, in whom I take refuge. He is my shield and the horn of my salvation, my stronghold.**
> **(Ps. 18:2)**

Will you take "responsibility?"

## A Bird's-Eye Before We Begin

Since folks are so busy and distracted these days, here's a bird's-eye view you can hang onto now, throughout our journey together, and beyond—until you see the earmarks of this truth in who you are for eternity:

1. The Weeping: In a broken world where suffering is unavoidable, all pain, trials, or "the free-falls of life" are providentially-allowed by God for the purposes of reminding us to see what the foundations of our life consist of—Creation, Christ, and Covenant...or some faulty set of beliefs, idols, vanities, or misconceptions. Trials are allowed, used by God as "pressure tests" of our most deeply held foundational beliefs, core values, non-negotiables of life.

## TAKE HEART

2. The Window: In Christ, once we're reminded of the fact that we're resting on the unshakable foundations of God's Creation, Christ, and Covenant, we can see the suffering is not about punishment, but purification: We're invited to take whatever time it takes to spend time looking into the window of our heart to discern the truths and falsehoods that we hold dear inside our heart— the repository of our faith. This "window of heart cleansing" won't stay open for long… Do not waste your heartbreak!

3. The Way: Before we turn back to face and help redeem the chaos of this broken life as changed, conformed, co-redeemers in Christ, we must get some very important things straight. As we will see, it's about Marking. Moaning. Marveling. And Moving—before we turn and intentionally walk into the chaos of brokenness where we're called to be Christ's claim, comfort, and compassion.

In short, God's consolation "Take Heart, Beloved!", and perfect plan for your pain, occurred in a miraculous way and is captured in "The Weeping, the Window, and the Way."

In the plain, I'm dyslexic: My near-term comprehension and memory are poor; I can tend to repeat myself; *but please hear this*: The repetition included in this book is purposeful and intentional. Honestly, respectfully-speaking, Take Heart is not a book for skimmers or "Christian light" reading, but rather for those who are tired of surface, shallow solutions to life's most shared, complicated, and plaguing question, "Will suffering make you bitter or better?" The offer, challenge ahead is will we "GoDeep!" to get at the answers? Please do.

*What Is Most Personal… The sacred, heartbreaking, and deeply personal time with my fatally wounded father on Christmas night offered me the crucial choice of faith: better over bitter.*

*Is Most Universal… Every human being will experience some form of suffering associated with living in a broken world. The choice is the same: Bitter or better?*

# 1

# The Christmas Crèche and Heartbreaking Crisis

Christmas night, 2002. The phone rang just as my family finished dinner. That single call would change my life forever.

"Johnny?" my stepmother, Marge, moaned on the other end of the line. "Johnny, I found a note from your dad. I think he's killed himself. Please come right away. Oh, God."

"Oh, G-G-God," I stammered my reply in a half-whisper to contain the shock that had just rifled through me. "Uh, yes, yes, I'll be right there."

Stunned, I put down the phone, choking back the flood of emotions that rushed into my throat from a place deep within my chest.

I drove to Dad's house, found him in the garden behind their home, and as I took hold of the doorknob and stepped out into the cold of night, my stomach jumped directly into my throat.

*JOHN O. DOZIER, JR.*

# Miraculous Moments

The moment I stepped outside—at that very moment in time—everything changed. Time and space took on a sense of otherness. Events slowed and seemed to stop, or nearly so. My need to be with Dad dissolved every other concern. I felt as though I had entered some kind of protective bubble. Maybe it was shock. Maybe I was momentarily deluded or hallucinogenic. Or maybe God had simply blessed me with the space and the time to be with my dad and with him, my Heavenly Father. I didn't know. But as I approached my Dad's body, I had a clear sense I had stepped into a place reserved specifically and especially for Dad, myself, and for one "other"—one who had not yet fully revealed himself to my senses. The spotlight in the garden seemed to be the only light in the entire world. The cold disappeared. Noises from the street, even the approaching sirens, sounded oddly muffled.

As if in slow motion, I fell to my knees, sobbing. "Oh, Dad. Oh, Dad. Oh, Dad." With each successive cry, I felt myself plummeting deeper and deeper. I was falling…and falling…and falling. Downward I fell with an ever-increasing sense of panic, a sense my free fall might never stop.

I rocked, fell, and wept. Nearly nauseous, I looked around me, desperate to find something solid, something on which to steady myself. I looked down—and saw Dad's favorite .9mm pistol lying next to him, under his right hip in the snow where he had fallen. Then I saw the blood pooled under his head. That's when I noticed Dad was still alive.

## TAKE HEART

He was shivering occasionally, barely breathing, and I had the distinct sense he was both "here yet not here" anymore.

On that tragic but transformative night, I cried out to God three times, and he answered with three sets of Scriptures—some known to me, some not, but all perfectly knit together to answer my questions of how a loving God could not only allow pain, but also use it to redeem those he loves. Don't you want to see your tragedies transformed?

As I continue to tell the story of my heart being stripped and hammered throughout the book, I hope you will see God's response to human suffering and his protocol for engaging and changing us through it. Like me, most of us don't begin with the questions of suffering; instead, they are thrust upon us in real life.

## Not If, but When

However it happens, our shared reality of suffering means that at some point all of us will ask the question: "If there really is an all-powerful and all-loving God, how can he allow such horrible and widespread suffering in the world? And in my life?" After all, if God loved me, how could he have me holding my dying father on Christmas night? Truthfully, if God didn't have a response to this most universal and personal question, he wouldn't be worthy of anyone's love and devotion! Beloved, it is impossible for God to be worthy on *any* level and not be with his Image Bearers at *every* level—but especially in the realms of dealing with the unavoidable suffering which accompanies living in a broken world.

Since we know we will experience suffering, the real question is: do we have the openness, humility, patience, and trust to hear God's response and live it out? In other words, will suffering make you bitter or better? These great, timely, and legitimate questions are not simply a philosophical debate but the real stuff of life, touching every moment of every day.

A God of such majesty and power must have a better way forward than simply "Suck it up and trust me!" Ultimately, it's not God who is lacking in providing us all the answers we need; it's us. It's you and me. We no longer know God well enough to really know his ways, to know how to trust him, and to know how to live fruitful lives in spite of all the hurt this fallen world throws at us, to know God's plan of redemption is far, far more than mere survival, pietistic self-help, or even healing: healing + resurrection = the purpose and freedom to be an increasingly conformed, Christ-like redemptive force in the world!

## The Christmas Crèche and a Heartbreaking Crisis

Our present pain is rooted in the past: The Fall (Genesis 3), when Adam and Eve chose to distrust and rebel against God rather than obey and love him. In that moment, the universe was broken in such a way that all current brokenness comes from that breaking, all falls from that Fall. Yet God, in his love, continues to use each heartbreak and free fall for our unique story and triumph. God is infinite yet intimate in all his marvelous and merciful ways.

## The Glory of God's Story: Creation, Fall, Redemption, Consummation

God has an amazingly grand plan in place. And if we're in Christ (John 3:16; 1 John 1:9) and know God's story, believe and have faith in it, embrace it, internalize it, feast on it in our hearts, pass it along to others whom God places in our life, wake up each day and go to bed each night reminding ourselves of it—life in this broken world will not only make much more sense but also be maxed out with meaning, purpose, indefatigable hope, radical downs, radical ups, and even more radical joy in the midst of it all.

God's story—all four "scenes," from Beginning to Consummation—is our story as well: in Christ, we now have the truest, most helpful perspective on how our origins were "very good" in the Beginning (Gen. 1:21), how it went very bad at the Fall (Gen. 3), how it was redeemed by the cross of Christ (1 John 1:9), and how it will all be made new when Christ returns to make it so (Rev. 22:12).

## JOHN O. DOZIER, JR.

*Creation: The Heart in the Beginning when everything was very good and as God meant it to be. In the beginning, Adam's heart bore the image of God's heart; the Garden of Eden was perfectly beautiful.*

## TAKE HEART

*The Fall: The Heart After the Fall: the tragic intrusion of sin and death, resulting in the pervasive brokenness of all people and everything God has made. Adam's heart, and all of mankind's inherited heart since then, was horribly marred and selfishly compartmentalized by the choice of being God—rather than allowing God to be God.*

JOHN O. DOZIER, JR.

*Redemption: The Heart and the Cross of Christ Within: God's astonishing promise to redeem his fallen image-bearers, humankind, and creation through the grace-filled work of his Son, Jesus Christ. The heart born-again through the Holy Spirit, real repentance, and in faith beseeching Christ to be our Savior and Lord, begins a journey as a new creation in Christ.*

## TAKE HEART

*Consummation: The Heart in the New Heaven and the New Earth: the magnificent fulfillment of God's Plan of Redemption to gather and cherish a people forever, and to live with them in a more-than-restored world, called "the new heaven and new earth." The heart of mankind restored to God's image and Eden-like state will indeed be one of the most glorious manifestations of God's redemptive plan.*

## A Take at Our Heart Story

Of course, in the beginning, it was not so. Suffering, pain, and death were completely foreign to God's creation and his intention for mankind. "In the beginning…" (Gen. 1:1), God spoke creation into existence and called each part of it "good." He culminated his work by creating man:

*Then God said, "Let us make man in our image, after our likeness. And let them have dominion over the fish of the sea and over the birds of the heavens and over the livestock and over all the earth and over every creeping thing that creeps on the earth." So God created man in his own image, in the image of God he created him; male and female he created them.*
*(Gen. 1:26–27)*

*Then the LORD God formed the man of dust from the ground and breathed into his nostrils the breath of life, and the man became a living creature.*
*(Gen. 2:7)*

Even though there is no explicit biblical evidence for my musings, I have long imagined God reaching down into the clay and forming Adam. He breathed life into his creation's nostrils and, with great delight, noticed Adam's heart, instantly animated, begin to beat. I imagine Adam's beautiful heart as the dominant feature of God's creative work, which initiated the creation of mankind. God made Adam's heart in his own image, albeit a "spirit image" (Gen. 5:1).

Then I imagine the Triune God smiling and, with deep satisfaction, celebrating with joy the "culmination and accumulation" of his now-completed work: the culmination in the form of Adam and the accumulation in the amassing of all the previous days' creative work. All taken together, this is something akin to the crescendo in God's marvelous creative symphony—the joy of this creative work within the Godhead:

> **God saw everything that he had made, and behold, it was very good. And there was evening and there was morning, the sixth day.**
> **(Gen. 1:37)**

Mankind surpasses in beauty any of the amazing arrays of wonders God had spoken into existence before Adam's creation. When God had finished creating all other things, he pronounced his creation "good"; after he formed and animated Adam, God declared his creation "very good." The emphasis in the Hebrew is intentional: God the Father, Son, and Holy Spirit could not have been more pleased!

## A Most Dreadful Change of Heart

Adam's heart, though finite, nevertheless mirrored the unblemished ecosystem of the infinite Creator's own heart in goodness, truth, wisdom, justice, holiness, mercy, patience, compassion, righteousness, and sacrificial love. Adam shared—though in a finite, limited way—God's own limitless beauty, his creativity, and his delight in him. Such was the heart of Adam in the beginning.

Adam's heart, like all of Creation, was perfectly created by God's love and truth. But please hear this: within the context of the definition of love, Adam was given a choice to love and obey God or not. Adam's free will choice "to love God back" had to exist, or God's consummate creation would be nothing more than a puppet. As we all know in storybook form, and hopefully in a real-life and personal form, Adam chose poorly. Sin entered into Adam's heart, and in the hearts of all mankind ever since (Gen. 3; Ps. 51:5). And this is a massive problem.

## Life in a Horribly Broken World

Our planet lives under the shroud that Adam's sin drew over humanity. Even Sunday school children know the story of Adam's rebellion and exile from Eden, but I invite you to look in a fresh way at the account, considering the "change of heart" that resulted from the first sin:

***The LORD God took the man and put him in the Garden of Eden to work it and keep it. And the LORD God commanded the man, saying, "You may surely eat of every tree of the garden, but of the tree of the knowledge of good and evil you shall not eat, for in the day that you eat of it you shall surely die."***
***(Gen. 2:15–17)***

***So when the woman saw that the tree was good for food, and that it was a delight to the eyes, and that the tree was to be desired to make one wise, she took of its fruit and ate, and she also gave***

***some to her husband who was with her, and he ate. Then the eyes of both were opened, and they knew that they were naked. And they sewed fig leaves together and made themselves loincloths. (Gen. 3:6–7)***

Adam's heart, the glorious culmination of God's creative act, changed immediately. Relationship with God, others, self, and Creation itself all broke in a single act. A moment earlier, it had mirrored God's own character, but now it was filled with doubts about God, self-trust and idolatry, shame, and fear. Gone were Eden's sweetest smells, its most glorious light, its freshest streams and most beautiful glades. Gone were the shameless nakedness and the joy of intimacy with God. Gone was the ability to worship God perfectly, freely, and within the realms of his own majestic love and truth.

The heart that turned from God died (Gen. 2:17), and Adam and Eve began the decline toward death in every realm, incrementally turning into a hardened, hiding, and decaying version of the clay from which God had formed them. Their hearts—now atrophying, scarred, and misshapen—no longer reflected the peace and joy the Creator had intended, and we, humankind, have all inherited that same enmity at God. Notice what comes next:

***The LORD saw that the wickedness of man was great in the earth, and that every intention of the thoughts of his heart was only evil continually. (Gen. 6:5)***

## *The heart is deceitful above all things, and desperately sick; who can understand it? (Jer. 17:9)*

Scripture paints a bleak picture of the unredeemed heart as the following:

- Bent, on suppressing the truth (Rom. 1:18–32; Eph. 4:19; 2 Pet. 2:14)
- Idolatrous, worshiping lesser gods (Lev. 26:30; Deut. 30:17; Exod. 20:1–7; Ezek. 11:21; Luke 16:15; 2 Thess. 3:5)
- "Lovers of themselves, lovers of money, boasters, proud, blasphemers, disobedient to parents, unthankful, unholy, unloving, unforgiving, slanderers, without self-control, brutal, despisers of good, traitors, headstrong, haughty, lovers of pleasure rather than lovers of God, having a form of godliness but denying its power" (2 Tim. 3:2–5)
- Uncircumcised (Jer. 9:26; Ezek. 44:7; compare with Acts 7:51)
- Hardened (Exod. 4:21)
- Wicked (Prov. 26:23)
- Perverse (Prov. 11:20)
- Godless (Job 36:13)
- "Split Spiritual Personality" (Rom. 7:15–20)

The Westminster Confession succinctly expresses the results of sin:

*By this sin they [Adam and Eve] fell from their original righteousness and communion with God, and so became dead in sin, and wholly defiled in all the parts and faculties of soul and body.*

## TAKE HEART

*They, being the root of all mankind, the guilt of this sin was imputed, and the same death in sin, and corrupted nature, conveyed to all their posterity [all human beings] descending from them by ordinary generation. From this original corruption, whereby we are utterly indisposed, disabled, and made opposite to all good, and wholly inclined to all evil, do precede all actual transgressions.*
*(The Westminster Confession, article 6:1–4)*

We are sinners not because we sin, but rather we sin because we are sinners. And therefore, as King David bemoans his state, "Surely I was sinful at birth, sinful from the time my mother conceived me" (Ps. 51:5).

## Suffering Flipped Upside Down by God— Father, Son, and Holy Spirit

Therefore, suffering originates from of the choices of Adam and Eve, but hear this: even though Adam and Eve's sin provided God full warrant to wipe out humanity, instead, he decided to *use* the sin and the brokenness of this world as a way to bring people (a) who do not believe in him to him for the first time and (b) the people who do believe closer and closer to the image of his Son, Jesus Christ. This is a huge part of God's plan of redemption, beloved: we deserve death, yet God provides not just life but a redeemed life—on a journey toward the likeness of his Son! This should bring us to our knees in thankfulness, joy, and witness. This is the *objective* truth of what God in the Trinity of Father, Son, and Holy Spirit—in unity, each with the same purpose yet differing roles—has brought about; the blessed offer, question is whether or not we will embrace it as a *subjective* reality in each of our lives.

This is an important reality to consider. God's love is so wide and deep that he has flipped the wholesale, utter brokenness of this world upside down, and rather than be the plight of all humankind, it is the path for humankind to come into relationship with God through repentance and the saving act of Jesus Christ on the cross, as well as the continued path of sanctification whereby we are conformed more and more into the likeness of Jesus Christ—in order to serve others and be "salt and light" in a decaying and dark world. It's how Paul can claim that we are "more than conquerors" (Rom. 8.37)!

In the next chapter, you will see the overview of how God's grace can work powerfully in your own life, suffering, and pain.

# 2

# We Can't Hear God's Protocol for Redemptive Suffering Enough

Christmas night 2002 was a tragic miracle. It was the night I found my father who lay dying shortly after his suicide. As I fell to my knees next my father, I cried out to God three times and amazingly received three miraculous responses from the Holy Spirit that form "God's protocol for redemptive suffering" outlined in this book—or the "Weeping, the Window, and the Way," previewed for you here:

*Every instance of pain or suffering creates a deep emotional response (Weeping) which leads to a magnificent view of God's grace and our own hearts (Window), and finally to the strength to move forward with renewed Christ-likeness and courage (Way).*

## The Weeping—Free Falls and Foundations

On Christmas night, when I knelt next to my mortally wounded father, I fell and fell and fell. I cried to God to stop the free fall of heartbreak and shock. The Spirit answered with, "In the beginning, God created the heavens and earth" (Gen. 1:1); "In the beginning was the Word" (John 1); and "Do not be afraid or discouraged because of them, the Lord your God will go with you, he will never leave you or forsake you" (Deut. 31:6). The free fall stopped, and I was kneeling on the unshakable foundations of Creation, Christ, and Covenant. I knew I could never sink beneath this rock-solid foundation.

## Application in brief

God allows little and big free falls to help us see what our foundations consist of and bring us back to God as manifest in his Creation, Christ, and Covenant.

## The Window—More Sinful and More Loved

Once I was resting on an unwavering and fixed foundation of the, and my, faith, I was racked by the true and false guilt for many things in my relationship between my father and me. Since I had already become a Christian, I knew this was not punishment (since that was "finished" (John 19:30), taken by Christ on the cross for me) but purification. The would-a, could-a, should-a's rolled in and down upon me like gigantic waves, each with crushing, searing pain. I cried out to God for the second time, and the Spirit answered with, "For the wrath of God is revealed from heaven against all ungodliness and unrighteousness of men, who by their unrighteousness suppress the truth" (Rom. 1:18) and "There is therefore now no condemnation for those who are in Christ Jesus" (Rom. 8:1). It was "the bookends of the Gospel": He laid bare the depth of my sin (Rom. 1:18) yet affirmed the heights of his love (Rom. 8:1).

*TAKE HEART*

## Application in brief

The Gospel reality of "More Sinful and More Loved" (while firmly resting on the foundations of Creation, Christ, and Covenant) frees us to peer into the window of our heart blown open by suffering. In any trial, we must throw off all restraints to look more and more deeply into our hearts to see what truths and falsehoods reside inside. This rare, glorious, and courageous time provides inventory of what inhabits our hearts, buried and compartmentalized within, and what exists there that loves God or hates him. Both exist: one blesses, the other condemns, but the truth sets us free.

## The Way—Moving Back into the Chaos, Redeemed to Redeem

When it was finally time to leave the side of my dying dad and enter the chaos that awaited, I was petrified. The oncoming shock, heartbreak, and screaming pain perfectly matched the glare of emergency vehicle lights reflecting off the Christmas night snow. For the final time, I cried out to God to give me strength to find a way back into the chaos and the shards of many broken hearts.

The Spirit answered me with, "I will give them one heart, and a new spirit I will put within them. I will remove the heart of stone from their flesh and give them a heart of flesh" (Ezek. 11:19); "We know that for those who love God all things work together for good, for those who are called according to his purpose" (Rom. 8:28); "Do not be conformed to this world, but be transformed by the renewal of your mind, that by testing you may discern what is the will of God, what is good and acceptable and perfect" (Rom. 12:2); "For I know that my Redeemer lives, and at the last he will stand upon the earth" (Job 19:25).

## Application in brief

These four passages, linked to one another, demonstrate one of the most important reasons why God uses suffering to sanctify the saints: we've been redeemed to redeem! Saved to serve. Comforted to comfort. Made holy to be wholly devoted to Jesus and his ministry. No manner or scope of chaos in this dark world is a match for Christ—in you and me—the hope of glory (Col. 1.26).

Take heart. God infinitely yet intimately orchestrates the unavoidable suffering of this broken world. He does so for his glory and purposes of bringing sinners to himself (in repentance and salvation) and then "back to himself over and over again" (for sanctification, which is conformation into the likeness of Jesus Christ, so we become the light and salt God intends). This is mercy beyond all compare.

We begin our lives "in Adam," with a heart of stone. By repentance, justification, and faith through Christ, our heart of stone is initially replaced in regeneration and repentance and then continually turned into a heart of flesh. From that point on, by means of Christ-centered obedience in Jesus's name, our heart is continually turned from stone into flesh—until we die or Jesus returns to make all things new (Rev. 21:5).

## TAKE HEART

# Foundations First: Have You Been Born Again?

The foundational question before we move forward is first whether you are (a) "in Christ" (2 Cor. 5:17; Gal. 3:26; 1 John 5:11–12) or (b) "outside of Christ" (John 3:3; Rom. 1:18–32; Eph. 2:8–9). Why? Because when it comes to God's plan to redeem all your lightest travails and darkest tribulations, whether or not you have been elected (Eph. 1:4–5), repentant (Acts 3:19), converted (Acts 2:38), born again (John 3:3), and have bona fide (Gal. 2:20) faith (Heb. 11:6) in the God of the Bible or not makes all the difference in the universe. Why? You cannot access the power and transformation of "The Weeping, Window, and Way" unless you have first been converted and submitted your life to Jesus Christ by repentance and faith by grace alone.

"First things last": sanctification follows salvation; spiritual adulthood follows adoption, spiritual infancy; consummation follows conversion; purification follows propitiation; maturity follows spiritual infancy; conformation follows re-creation; beautification follows being made new.

# Or Living Outside Christ

Though I aim to speak the truth in love, this leads us to a hard reality: if you have yet to place your faith in the God of the Bible, you really have no warrant to complain, lash out in anger, be perplexed and confused, or blame God for suffering (or anything) in any way. Why? Devoid of real, living, and active faith in God, our only three choices are the following: (1) to relent to the blind misfortune of happenstance and be stoic ("it's a dog eat dog world," "survival of the fittest," "have a stiff upper lip"); (2) deny reality and pain exist and be an existentialist (life is meaningless, but I strive on), and/or (3) avoid pain by embracing all sorts of pleasure that distracts and be a hedonist (living for the gratification of physical/sensual desires).

As the book of Ecclesiastes says, if God is meaningless to you, you are a "functional atheist." The only choices are *stoicism*, *existentialism*, or *hedonism*—and these are no way to live your precious life. This response has some logical legitimacy, but it's just so utterly counter to every molecule in our being, which craves a much deeper, truer, lovelier, and more satisfying answer—one only God can provide. We must first be changed from the *inside-out* before we can deal with life's joys and/or brokenness that come at us from the *outside-in*.

If you are "outside of Christ"—not having repented in desperation after seeing God's holiness, your own sin, and the unbridgeable expanse in between—then your stony heart is yet to be regenerated and "from stone to flesh" (Ezek. 36:26). Ergo, "God's protocol for redemptive suffering" cannot occur, meaning your suffering will lead you to be bitter rather than better. We must first be *saved* in order to be *sanctified*, purified, conformed, and sent into the world as Jesus' light and salt.

## TAKE HEART

Has your heart been redeemed? Have you repented and come to Christ to receive his gift of free grace? If not, please consider faith in Christ "today" (Ps. 95:7–8; 2 Cor. 6:2).

If, on the other hand, you can mark a period of your life where you repented of your sin and knew your conversion had occurred, you have begun the journey of Christ-likeness whereby your suffering can have the effect that God ordained as we trust him and the process. When we are converted, the Holy Spirit begins the process before we are even aware of it by regenerating our dead, stony heart into a heart of flesh that becomes alive and new, a heart that gives us confidence of God's ability to use our suffering to make us holy, mature, joyful, purposeful, and useful (Eph. 2:1–10, Rom. 8:28). That new heart is so powerful it even allows us to do the following:

***Count it all joy, my brothers, when you meet trials of various kinds, for you know that the testing of your faith produces steadfastness. And let steadfastness have its full effect, that you may be perfect and complete, lacking in nothing. (James 1:2–4)***

Don't miss this: the existence and increase of *all joy* that James is referring to does not usually happen immediately upon conversion—it's the fruit (and the increase of it) of remaining steadfast and faithful in the midst of the unavoidable suffering we will all experience while living in a broken world. The joy James is promoting is about conformation: becoming more and more like Jesus.

*JOHN O. DOZIER, JR.*

# Take Pause: Being Sanctified Is Preceded by Being Saved

Please pause right now with a trusted Christian. Search your heart about the "line of faith," which you may or may not have crossed. Have you been born again? How did your conversion occur? If you were to die and face Jesus today, how would you respond to his questions: "Who do you say I am? Why should I allow you into My kingdom?"

Today may be the day of your salvation in or recommitment to Christ and further purification through your trials. Search your heart now and ask God to search it too. This is why the psalmist so persistently and passionately implores God:

***Search me, O God, and know my heart; test me and know my anxious thoughts. See if there is any offensive way in me, and lead me in the way everlasting.***
***(Ps.139:23–24)***

This is the prayer of a person who understands the deep need we all share to have our hearts radically restored—first by being born again and then by being discipled, refined, matured, sanctified, and conformed into the likeness of Jesus for service to others in his name. This prayer embraces "the weeping, the window, and the way" as God's healing work in the human heart, his protocol for using the inevitable trials of this life to work in his faith-filled people wholehearted love for God and the ability to bless others (Exod. 20; Matt. 22:34–40; 2 Cor. 1:3–7).

## TAKE HEART

As you examine and pray, know that we are never freer than when we are frail and on our knees, "heartbroken and wide open" before a merciful God (and, perhaps, also a committed Christian friend) who cares deeply for our heart. As a way to do this "heart exam," ask, "Have I?" for the following:

a) Considered the utter holiness of God?
b) Faced the impossibility of my standing face to face with a holy God who cannot tolerate any sin?
c) Understood I cannot cover the indelible stain of my own sin?
d) Humbly responded by repenting from the depth of my heart and asking Jesus Christ to save me from God's just condemnation and be the Lord of my life?
e) Tasted the sweetness that comes from trusting God's character/promise to love me as he does his own Son?
f) Set a course for discipleship and mission to follow Jesus and serve others?

You are far from alone; every person on the planet falls into one or the other category. The Bible is explicit that there are only "two races of people"—those who have faith in him, and those do not (Heb. 11:6; John 8:24). Please choose and/or recommit this day (Josh. 24:15).

# 3

# Living in a Culture of Comfort

*"If you have a Christian faith that is not shot through with reason and thinking, that faith will not last through all of the up's and down's of life."*
*(Pastor Timothy Keller, 9/11 Sermon: Truth, Tears, Anger and Grace, September 16, 2001)*

If you are a Christian, that means you have a deep-rooted desire to see your heart be transformed to mirror the heart of your namesake, Jesus Christ, by any means necessary—yes, even and especially the means of suffering. In other words, *you want Jesus more than you want comfort.* Why do we squirm, twist, and turn in every which direction to avoid engaging God's process of "The Weeping, the Window, and the Way?" What inhibits even most believers from more fully embracing the ideas we've considered in this book thus far?

Westernized, twenty-first century Christians live in a precarious predicament. We enjoy so many advantages—advantages beyond the wildest imagination of most people who have ever lived on our planet throughout all the centuries and millennia up to now. Most of these advantages still today lie well beyond the grasp of the majority of humanity. Yet these advantages represent a very mixed blessing, a blessing I like to call our "culture of comfort."

## "Theodicy" Is Going Unanswered by the Steward of God's Aim and Answer: The Church

Measures of this claim concerning the question of theodicy going unanswered can be seen in a host of ways, ranging from the alarming number of Christians who cannot biblically or personally answer the question of theodicy ("How can an all-powerful and all-loving God allow suffering?") to an inability to deal with even a minimal of messy problems in the church, problems that grow from bad to worse as they remain undealt with. And far worse still, the world of unbelievers—for whom the church is called to be the truth-revealing light and decay-stemming salt for—names as the number 1 reason why they remain steadfast skeptics, agnostics, or atheists is the existence of a God who apparently cares so little about such widespread and horrid suffering in the world. This reality is a very big problem for the church—God's answer for life's most daunting and everyday questions.

Comfort begets comfort until even the most benign paper cut to the emotions sends alarms. So we hide and/or harden, and then not only do the deeper problems never get raised or resolved but also the consequential increase of spiritual and emotional ambivalence naturally, organically results in such a state of compartmentalization and bifurcated, divergent thinking that we can and do "go insane": doing the same wrong-hearted and wrong-headed things over and over while expecting a different outcome. Cut off from the taproot of redemptive suffering, we just suffer until we get insufferable.

The writer of Hebrews compares Jesus's "alien, estranged nature" and "attached detachment" to this world, traits we are supposed to emulate in joyful obedience (Acts 5:29; 1 Pet. 1:14):

> ***Therefore, let us go to him [Jesus] outside the camp and bear the reproach he [Jesus] endured. For here we have no lasting city, but we seek the city that is to come.***
> ***(Heb.13:13–14)***

Happily, this is nothing new; God's people have faced this before, and his Scripture is sufficient. God has chosen us to be set apart from the world, even as we share his forgiveness and hope with the world. God has sent us into this world, yet not of it, and commissioned us to carry out his mission here. The entire Bible story is about an "intervention from the outside" as the first cause and final cure.

## The Church's Wake-Up Call

As such, the church must intervene as well. Yet in the world, we have often fallen prey to the temptation to let the world be too thoroughly in us. In a variety of ways, we have allowed its influence to mute our passion for God's mission and to derail the tasks he has given us for bringing his vision to life. Whenever God's people have adapted to the local culture, we have become worldly, lightless, saltless, helpless, and hopeless. Over the past few decades, Christians in the Western world have grown more comfortable with and even part of the "culture of comfort." We have made it our whole purpose in life to avoid one thing: discomfort.

## Don't Get Comfy Here!

God made us for more than worldly comfort. Scripture again and again describes the normal Christian life as anything but a life of ease:

> *And not only this, but we also exult in our tribulations, knowing that tribulation brings about perseverance; and perseverance, proven character; and proven character, hope; and hope does not disappoint, because the love of God has been poured out within our hearts through the Holy Spirit who was given to us.*
> *(Rom.5:1–5, NIV)*

> *In this you greatly rejoice, though now for a little while you may have had to suffer grief in all kinds of trials. These have come so that your faith—of greater worth than gold, which perishes even though refined by fire—may be proved genuine and may result in praise, glory and honor when Jesus Christ is revealed.*
> *(1 Pet. 1:3–7, NIV)*

## TAKE HEART

***But rejoice insofar as you share Christ's
sufferings, that you may also rejoice and be glad
when his glory is revealed.
(1 Pet. 4:12–13)***

God tells us to rejoice in our suffering. Conversely, the Bible warns God's people again and again against the dangers of adopting the culture of the world system around us:

***[Jesus said,] "If you were of the world, the world
would love you as its own; but because you are
not of the world, but I chose you out of the world,
therefore the world hates you."
(John 15:19)***

***Now we have received not the spirit of the world,
but the Spirit who is from God, that we might
understand the things freely given us by God.
And we impart this in words not taught by human
wisdom but taught by the Spirit, interpreting
spiritual truths to those who are spiritual.
(1 Cor. 2:12–13)***

## God Infinitely and Intimately Loves Your Heart

Out of deep love for our hearts, God warns urgently against adopting the values of a culture of comfort and worldliness because of the very real dangers it poses. Remember, he notices when one downy feather falls from a bird's wing or a blade of grass quakes in the wind (Luke 12:22–31). Not only that, he sent his own Son to die for us! Surely he does not allow his own elect redeemed sons and daughters to suffer pointless pain.

Rather, he uses the weeping and heartbreak we experience in a sinful, broken, and persecuting world to protect us from the dangers of a culture that opposes his salvation and work and to refine our hearts into the temperament of Jesus himself, the Ultimate Intervener and Cosmic Cure. He "suffered not so that we would not suffer, but so that when we do suffer, we become more like him" (Keller). Strikingly, Calvin says,

> *Because we are so inclined to put our own comfort and advantage first and avoid adversity… Our most merciful Father comforts us by this teaching: that he promotes our salvation [and sanctification\*] by inflicting the cross upon us. [\*What Calvin calls "furthering our salvation."] (John Calvin)*

**Do not love the world or the things in the world. If anyone loves the world, the love of the Father is not in him. For all that is in the world—the desires of the flesh and the desires of the eyes and pride in possessions—is not from the Father but is from the world. And the world is passing away along with its desires, but whoever does the will of God abides forever.**
**(1 John 2:15–17)**

## Getting to the Heart of the Matter: It's a Matter of the Heart

In short, the culture of comfort creates a toxic hiding and hardening environment for the human heart. When we

# TAKE HEART

allow Christ to tenderly care for our discomfort, our hearts soften. But when we unknowingly allow the world system, our own sinful flesh, or the devil himself to anesthetize and suppress our discomfort, it's the hardening process itself that makes us more comfortable, which is another way of saying that the "comfort" we experience comes from death—death of heart and spirit, of our "selves," as God intended us to be. Our heart and our witness become exactly like the impermeable rock-encased cross in the stone that I found as a ten-year-old boy.

*While hiding, playing in the creek near our home, I broke a hard, reddish-maroon rock perfectly in half with another, larger rock.*

Despite the discomfort he knows we will experience, God always intends his weeping/window/way protocol for redemptive suffering—to be for our good, for our "very good" (Gen. 1:31). He knows when we attempt to avoid the weeping, we doom ourselves to the same state of heart experienced by the author of Ecclesiastes:

> ***"Meaningless! Meaningless!" says the Teacher. "Utterly meaningless! Everything is meaningless…under the sun."***
> ***(Eccles. 1:2, NIV)***

Beloved, God made us for so much more than "meaninglessness." He made us to be agents of his redemption and transformation for the whole Creation. Therefore, even in our pain, we can—we really and truly can and should—take heart.

# 4

# Take Heart!

Biblically speaking—which is all that really matters—Take Heart reminds us that the heart of the matter is a matter of the heart. It's vitally important we take time to see how the Bible defines our heart. I promise you, we're going to get into some practical application about how best to handle any and all hurts, but doing so devoid of the "big-picture" truths will not simply make the details more elusive and ineffective: it will leave them greatly diluted and diminished of the healing power God, you, so desperately want and need.

## Getting to the Heart of the Heart

*No secrets of the heart and mind remained hidden when Jonathan Edwards called for self-scrutiny, this meant the relentless need to distinguish between the true and false affections; between those affections having to do with a redeemed heart, and those darkened by sin. To clarify these distinctions was Edwards' purpose in his life and in seeing the Great Awakening come to pass.*
*(Harold Simonson)*

Scripture calls King David "a man after God's own heart" (1 Sam. 13:13–14), though he faced the same temptations you and I face each day. When confronted with his most grievous sin of adultery, he dropped to his knees and confessed, "Against you [God], you only, have I sinned and done what is evil in your sight" (Ps. 51:4). David's weeping and penitential prayer serves as a powerful example for us. He recognized the internal cause of his external sins, the "sin beneath the sins," that had dethroned God and had made adultery and murder first possible, then attractive, and finally consummated.

The word heart and its various synonyms show up in the Bible over 2,500 times. Does that tell you something about the high priority God places on your heart? Does it compel you to consider how high a priority you place on the true nature and condition of your own heart? When I first came to realize and understand this emphasis in Scripture and began to discern the distinction between the heart and the spirit, it radically transformed my perspective. How important it is that we give our hearts the kind of focused attention God gives them, the kind of scrutiny Jonathan Edwards recommended in the quote above.

Seen yet another way, when in the Bible Jesus says, "Love God with your whole heart, mind, soul, and strength" (Luke 10:27), he's placing three times the emphasis on our "soul, heart, mind" than he is on our "strength," or the free will we're imbued with to carry out life. The Bible repeatedly tells us if our heart is in the right place, our actions will follow. (And the opposite is also true.) You see, "soul, heart, mind" have so much overlap in the Bible that simply saying, "Guard your heart, for it is the wellspring of life" (Prov. 4:23) will do.

What the Bible calls the "heart"—which, as we have and will see, in biblical usage—does not mean feelings or emotions, as we often use the word heart today. But rather, it is the heart that encompasses the entire feeling, thinking, and soulful being. It's the animating center of the human being that drives all we do—it was created by God very good (Gen. 1:21) and then went very bad (Gen. 3; Rom. 1:18-32). God's plan of redemption is all about remaking the heart—and all else in the universe—very good, even better than it was in the beginning, again.

## The Heart of the Matter: Good News to Everyone Who Believes

In God's realm, the heart is the seat of the entire self. It includes our worldview, our core values and commitments, our idealized image of how the world should be, and our non-negotiables. This is why the Bible exhorts us, "Above *all* else, guard your heart, for it is the wellspring of life" (Prov. 4:23, emphasis added).

What matters to God is the human heart (soul, mind)—the body too is important, will be raised but is secondary—as it reflects the state of the heart. As the revivalist preacher, philosopher, and Congregational Protestant theologian—and master of diagnosing humanity's makeup by how God created mankind and we image bearers are designed to glorify him—Jonathan Edwards wisely said of the soul/heart,

*The soul/heart is what is united to Christ. It is the soul/heart that is regenerated. It is the soul/heart that has its very nature changed. It is the soul/heart that is renewed and conformed into the image of Christ. It is the soul/heart that rejoices and grieves. The soul/heart*

*does not choose one or the other philosophical, moral paths from a state of neutrality; the soul/heart actively chooses one path or another based upon what it loves, and cannot do otherwise. (Dane Ortlund, Edwards on the Christian Life, WJE, 13:219-20; 14:295; Ibid; 17:135; 2:98; 22:363-62).*

As we will see, this should get under why God's sovereign and loving use of suffering is focused on a change of heart: a change for choosing based upon God's true truth and love and not the falsehoods of the world, the flesh, or the devil; a change for the betterment or—if suffering is suppressed, compartmentalized, and unused—a change for the embitterment of our heart.

What is your heart's default mode? What, who does your heart love? What do you think about when you are experiencing no pressure to think about anything else? Of what do your daydreams consist? What ideas, hopes, and ambitions most regularly compete for ascendancy in your heart? What do you most hope to accomplish? For what would you practically die to achieve/get?

Pause for a moment right now. Before you go on, think it through. In your heart of hearts, on what do you focus? In the margin of this book, finish this sentence "If only I…" Though the actual words may vary, most answers may sound strikingly similar to yours.

## Aspirations, Affections, and Exponential Complications

When God is not seated squarely in the center of our hearts, then just like a black hole in outer space, all else besides God will rush into the vacuum. Nature abhors a vacuum. Chaos, pain, guilt, fear, internal conflict, shame, anxiety, and all the other fruit of misplaced priorities result. Always. Where the God of the Bible does not reign, all forms of lesser gods will rush in to take God's place of preeminence within our heart. Seated in God's stead, idols will demand as much as God does but not offer any of God's mercy when we fail to worship the idol(s)—and fail over and over we will.

St. Augustine once defined sin as "making a good thing, the only or ultimate thing."

Satan cleverly uses "good things made ultimate things" to tempt us into worshiping the creation rather than the Creator. Since Satan the Deceiver has no original creative power in himself whatsoever, he must borrow God's good things to do what he does best: deceive, distract, delude, and eventually destroy any who might worship God.

The heart is meant to be the throne room of God only. God made your heart; his preeminence there is well deserved, and God knows we can only live a joyous and fulfilled life with him on the throne. If we get this even halfway right, we will come to see our pain as God painstakingly reminding us (not creating the pain, or pointing pain at us, but sovereignly using the pain of a broken world) of exactly who our hearts were made to worship. He is passionate about revealing to us the true nature of our hearts so that we might know ourselves well, and in knowing our need, we might throw ourselves on the salvation Jesus won for us on his cross and the sanctification faithfully following him provides.

Now we come to the word *spirit*, also linked to our hearts. In the Old Testament, the word spirit (Hebrew, ruwach) is equivalent to "wind." In the New Testament, the word spirit refers to our emotions or affections. Please get a hold of this: our emotions are linked directly to those things we treasure as most important to our well-being; *they link directly to the things of the heart*—our worldview, hopes, dreams, core beliefs, values, non-negotiables, and deepest desires. If our heart is, according to God's standards, "in the right place," our emotional homeostasis, stability, "fruit" will be good as well (Gal. 5:22–23). But if our heart has wandered away from, or is in conflict with God's will and standards for our life, our emotional makeup will reflect it in a host of negative and destructive ways (Gal. 5:19–21). Or, put another way, look up the antonyms, opposites of each of the Fruit of the Spirit.

As Jesus, the maker and lover of our heart, said, "How can you speak good, when you are evil? For out of the abundance of the heart the mouth speaks" (Matt. 12:34, emphasis added).

**For from within, out of the heart of man, come evil thoughts, sexual immorality, theft, murder, adultery, coveting, wickedness, deceit, sensuality, envy, slander, pride, foolishness. All these evil things come from within, and they defile a person.**
**(Mark 7:21–23)**

## TAKE HEART

Each and every person whom God has created clings to a different set of "essential things" within their heart. These, in turn, link directly to various sets of emotions or feelings that surround, guide, guard, and defend each truth or falsehood of the heart. This creates individuality and uniqueness among all God's children, a uniqueness that God uniquely knows and cherishes—so much, in fact, that he sent his Son to redeem them.

Bottom line: the heart is complicated. And not treating it as such can be as disastrous as not recognizing it at all. But also get this: things can be a great deal less complicated if we can see, embrace, and steward "the ecosystem of our heart-spirit-life." So there is a choice before you to slow down, take heart, and experience God's transformation, or do nothing and watch your heart hide and harden before you.

I'm afraid the choice to remain in between is only an embittered and faithless life (Mark 16:16) or the lukewarm life (Rev. 3:16). Please choose this day to not be hardened or lukewarm anymore. As a man whose heart has been transformed in and by this process of "God's protocol for redemptive suffering," I long to see others experience the same.

If we will be intentional about filling our hearts with God's Bible-based love and truth, our emotional health and well-being—the increase and growth of our ability to have more love, joy, peace, patience, kindness, goodness, faithfulness, gentleness, and self-control—will occur. Why? Because that is the fruit of the Spirit (Gal. 5:22–23) who is living, growing, softening the heart, pointing to Jesus, and flourishing inside. The Holy Spirit is The Supernatural Heart-Changer!

## The Heart and Its "Precious"

In J. R. R. Tolkien's masterful trilogy The Lord of the Rings, the once-Hobbit Sméagol accidentally finds the One Ring belonging to the Dark Lord Sauron. He takes it for his own, commits murder to keep it, and rapidly transforms into a monstrous version of himself—Gollum. Rejected by his community and family, he follows a path into the Misty Mountains and disappears into a cave, taking the One Ring with him.

The ring has the potential to make Gollum godlike in knowledge and control, and he spends five hundred years underground consumed by thoughts of it. Helplessly isolated with his heart torn in pieces by his choices, Gollum flees farther and farther into the heart of darkness, away from anyone who would scheme to steal the ring, which he calls his Precious. Again and again, he repeats the mantra, "My Precccioussss…" He is helplessly held in bondage by his idolatrous fascination with power and control and tortured by an internal tug-of-war.

Tolkien saw the truth clearly: idols will incrementally and utterly destroy human hearts. Gollum's "Precious" took up residence in a place meant only for God's residence and rule. It demanded as much as God did but without bestowing any of the mercy, forgiveness, or joy a relationship with him brings. Yet despite the anguish they cause, the allure of pride, the mystery of power, and the illusion of control tugs at every human heart.

As a result, our "split personality," our isolation and pain lurk just below the veneer of everyone's behavior. For example, when people are asked how they are doing, most quickly respond with a simple "Fine" or "Really busy." Much of the time, however, this response masks the truth and silences a desperate voice inside that is really crying, "Help! My heart is breaking about something today, but I can't let it show. I'm too prideful, ashamed, wounded, alienated, or fearful of my emotions to let you know."

No one is immune. If our hearts stop worshipping God, we don't worship nothing—we will worship anything. Our hearts must have a Precious. What gods are you holding as Precious? Will you take the time to examine your heart, truly ask that question, and consider inviting another person to walk with you along the way?

## Pause. Breathe. Slow (Way) Down: Even if It's Super Hard

There is hardly anything in our fast-paced culture and busy-sick lives that compels us to slow down and take a deep breath, is there? Nonetheless, I'm pleading with you right now to consider doing so. Intentionally set aside a time and place of peace and quiet, or a chunk of each day. The early morning and desolate wilderness were biblical times and places, some secluded place where the deafening din of daily noise can't get to you. It's good to do this alone but vital to do it with a fellow Christian as well: the community of faith is meant to promote clearer thinking, accountability, speaking truth in love to one another—all for the purposes of renewing our commitment to be ambassadors of Christ.

As I said before, you will know which gods are precious by asking, "What do I daydream about? Where does my mind go when I have nothing else to do? What am I afraid to lose? What do I have to have for my life to be complete, valid, or satisfied?" If we don't do this work, we will end with a hardened and compartmentalized heart, a war of emotions we can't cope with, and a meaningless life.

It's well worth repeating: we will inevitably choose one of the three previously mentioned worldviews explored in Ecclesiastes, which I am fervently praying you avoid. Tragically, each injects an equally potent spiritual poison which will harden the human heart:

- Stoicism. A lifestyle that denies or avoids emotions, considering them irrelevant. Stoics deal with "destructive emotions" by means of extreme self-control and inner fortitude.
- Hedonism. Stoicism's opposite, this lifestyle focuses on experiencing as much unrestrained pleasure as possible, considering pleasure to be life's chief (or sole) end.
- Existentialism. A lifestyle that grows out of despair based on the belief that existence has no purpose or meaning but puts on a brave front and faces daily life with courage, and even lofty convictions,

despite deep despair, "the existential angst" of meaninglessness piled on each and every day.

Are any of these "isms" familiar to you? In contrast to these toxic approaches to life's hurts, God calls his people to share in Christ's sufferings. Our tears do not surprise God. Our weeping serves as the engine in God's redemptive plan to bring his kingdom "on Earth as in Heaven" and to make us more fully fit for kingdom citizenship.

## Take Hope

Before more of the delights and details of how God has so markedly and mercifully provides for our heartbreak(s), please enjoy a feast of the heart of God's promises in and for your pain—a feast that we pass up at the risk of forever hardening our heart. A biblical response to suffering or trials of any kind will:

- motivate us to prayer (Ps. 30);
- increase our trust in the person, providence, and power of God (Ps. 119:71; 2 Cor. 12:5, 9, 10);
- train us in obedience, patience, and hope (Rom. 5; Heb. 1);
- promote sanctification (moving closer to holiness, purity, growth) (Prov. 3:11–12; John 17:17; Rom. 8:28; 1 Cor. 11:32; Heb. 12:8; 13:12);
- conform us more and more into the likeness of Jesus Christ (Prov. 66:10; Rom. 8:29; 12:2; Heb. 2:10);

- increase joy, wisdom, and meaning within our heart (Rom. 11:33–34; James 1; Col. 1:24);
- teach us compassion for other sufferers (Ps. 72:12; 2 Cor. 1:3–7; James 1:27);
- increase the depth and breadth of the fruit of the spirit (Matt. 3:8; John 12:24; Gal. 5);
- offer manifold opportunities of seeing God's glory and people's blessing as we move through the trial and not around it (Ezek. 11:18–21; Luke 24:26; 2 Cor. 1:5; Phil. 3:8; 1 Pet. 5);
- humble us while prying our fingers off the perishable things of this passing world (Ps. 39:6; 1 Cor. 7:31; 2 Cor. 12:7; 1 Pet. 1:24);
- teach us to bear one another's burdens and live in community (Gen. 48:4; Heb. 13; Rom. 1:12; Col. 2:2; Gal. 6:2); and
- set our heart on the hope and assurance of eternal glory (Jer. 29:11; Rom. 5:2–5).

## Take Heart

*For this light, momentary affliction is preparing for us an eternal weight of glory beyond all comparison, as we look not to the things that are seen but to the things that are unseen. For the things that are seen are transient, but the things that are unseen are eternal.*
*(2 Cor. 4:17–18)*

From the rubble of our broken world and sinful lives, God calls us to a lifelong journey of faith intended to rearrange the ecosystem of our hearts so that we become more and more like Jesus. This divine protocol by which God uses our heartbreaks in redemption to draw us closer to himself, I have called "the weeping, the window, and the way." I believe this is the process by which God reforms our hearts to make us more and more like Christ himself for the express purpose of being co-redeemers sent on a mission by, through, and with him. We who are in Christ are reborn to help others make the invisible visible and the visible viable so that we glorify God and live and love more like his Son.

As we will see in more detail later on, trials of any kind offer us an array of benefits that, if shunned, condemn each one of us to a living hell. Counterintuitive, right? How could suffering of any kind reflect anything *but* hell? The answers to such a question should never be blindly shrouded under "God's great mysteries" but rather stewarded for the sake of the world.

Sadly, the stewardship of these answers is in the hands of a church that, in many cases, stands just as confused, wounded, and silent as the world. This is indeed a crime, a crime I do not stand in judgment of but rather am in tears about. It is time for the church—and for each of us as members of the Body of Christ—to reorient, renovate, recount, renew, redirect, and revitalize our understanding and redemptive use of suffering. It's time for us to get back to radical involvement in God's redemptive plan for his world. Those who avoid the weeping will never benefit from the opportunity for repentance, for growth in grace, and for the self-sacrificial service God has graciously designed into the fabric of our suffering. These missed opportunities sadden God and hurt us.

For the next three chapters, I am going to share the story of Christmas night 2002, seen in three sets of passages I received from God by the person of the Holy Spirit, after I fell to my knees by my dying father in the Christmas-night snow. My own experiences with the weeping, the window, and the way before that night, and after it was over, stripped away much of my pride and pretense, but not nearly all. I still seek more radical change of heart, spirit, and life even now.

My personal outcries to God on Christmas night were because of my personal experience of suffering and a heart-crushing experience. It was not long after I recorded the details of this miraculous exchange between myself and God I knew beyond a doubt it was not only for me (Rom. 15:1). None of God's numerous gifts are given for any of us alone but are to be given away (2 Cor. 1:3–7; Phil. 2; imitating Christ's humility and radical generosity).

If you pay careful attention to the principles and practices of each of the following three steps in "God's protocol for redemptive suffering," you will see God will be greatly glorified, you will be greatly blessed, and those around you will experience the redemptive power of the Triune God we so thank and adore. Of course, if you want to explore any of the content we will share together in this booklet by means of my original book, I would encourage you to do so.

# 5

# The Weeping:
# Free Falls and Foundations

Applying Genesis 1:1, John 1:1,
and Deuteronomy 31:6

**STEP 1. ALL WEEPING, ALL TEARS, ALL TRIALS, AND ALL FREEFALLS ARE GOD'S OFFER FOR REVEALING AND FIRMING UP THE FOUNDATIONS OF OUR FAITH.**

## JOHN O. DOZIER, JR.

*Freefalls: All weeping, trials, freefalls of life, results in a "freefall of faith" and the opportunity to know for the first time, or re-establish, the foundations of The Faith.*

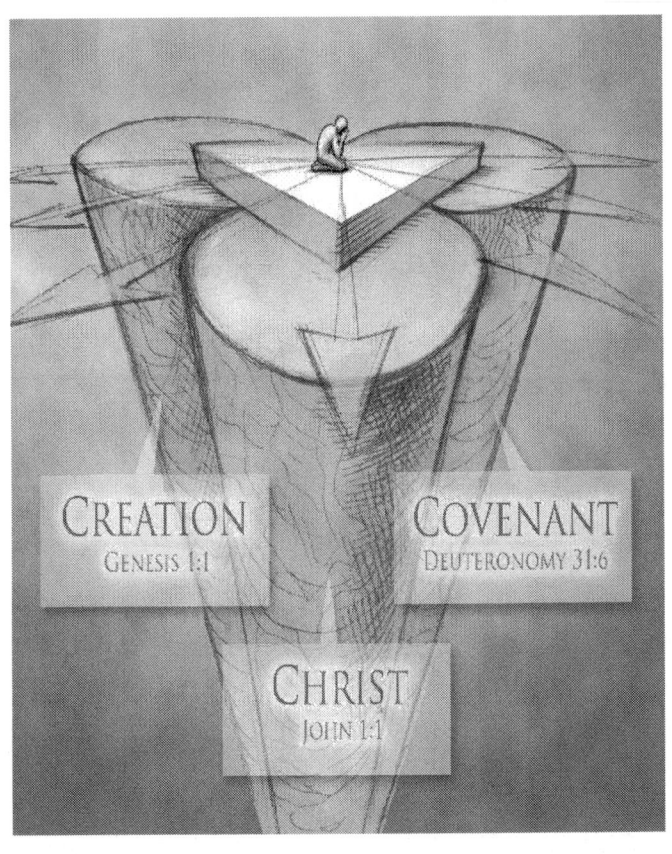

*Foundations: No human being can be fully human without foundations of some kind. And no worldview except a Biblical worldview offers a foundation of faith that is rationale, personal, universal, and grace-full.*

## JOHN O. DOZIER, JR.

*Believer, you have been radically changed and your life has been placed, by God's grace, on solid rock.*
*(Pastor Alistair Begg)*

## Crisis Happens

In response to his jawbone-cancer diagnosis, my father carefully planned to take his life on Christmas night 2002, with maximum family in town to support his wife, Margie, after his tragic choices. While my wife, Peggy; myself; our children Polly and Teddy; and Peggy's parents were having Christmas-night dinner, I received the life-shattering phone call that my father had shot himself. I fled the house, rushed to his side, and fell to my knees next to him in the snow.

## Family and Story: What's Most Personal Is Most Universal

Of course my story didn't start there. It began, as all stories do, with God. God is the greatest writer and storyteller in the universe. This means we all have a story, which helps us see how our stony hearts are formed. Remember, the heart is the center of your emotions, desires, and actions. The heart is at the center of God's promise, "And I will give them one heart, and put a new spirit within them; And I will take the heart of stone out of their flesh and give them a heart of flesh" (Ezek. 11:19; Jer. 24:7; Matt. 22:37; 2 Cor. 5:17). It occurs once at our conversion and then "over and over" in our discipleship, sanctification, and obedience, and, ultimately, in our being Christ-like. To truly meet God in our pain, we need to know our story because all of us have weeping in our childhoods.

*"And I will give them one heart, and a new spirit I will put within them. I will remove the heart of stone from their flesh and give them a heart of flesh"*
*(Ezekiel 11:19).]*

## JOHN O. DOZIER, JR.

As I tell my story—for the purpose of context and encouraging you to know and tell your own story—I am painfully aware that in doing so, I risk breaking an unspoken family pact—a pact of secrecy, silence, and even shame. I grew up in a spiritually misguided, addictive, and emotionally damaging family, and as all the literature on codependency will tell you, addictive and dysfunctional families keep secrets. No one has a perfect childhood. All families are flawed—some in one way, some in another—but knowing our own stories well is one initial key to experience God's healing.

As a young child, I endured some very painful wounds to the heart. Criticism, shame, and a dreadful sense of anonymity in my own home deeply damaged my heart and led to deep darkness and despair from an early age. It's clear my parents did not set out deliberately to pummel my heart and spirit, but having been raised in similarly heart-crushing environments, they were incapable of making different choices in raising my two sisters and me. Our story—and the stories of those who have shaped our story—is vitally important to know and to place our life into reality and some sort of context.

Mom grew up in an abusive, legalistic family and church. When finally freed from this repressive and oppressive environment by marriage, she set out to live—to really live—for the first time in her young life. Mom's insatiable appetite for life, created in part by a childhood that had not allowed her to express it, made it almost inevitable she would approach almost every circumstance, every relationship, every opportunity with questions like, "What does this have to do with me? With my dreams? With my agenda? With my as-yet-unfilled needs? With my pent-up desire to simply enjoy the heck out of life?"

Little did I know then, but the pattern of Mom's early life was the perfect setup for her to become inordinately focused on her own needs. The resulting narcissism was near-pathological and nastily punishing.

Mom's newfound freedom came at a price: the double dose of shame and guilt created in her heart by her childhood experiences and by her attempts to throw off the restraints had to be mollified. So she brokered an agreement first with herself by "shifting the shame and guilt" onto my siblings and me and then with God, forcing my sisters and me to participate in the same often doctrinally abusive and legalistic church she had endured in childhood.

For me, church provided no more solace than I had experienced at home. Week by week, my heart experienced the same kinds of criticism, shame, and anonymity I felt in my own home. But in church, God himself seemed to be the one pummeling my heart and spirit. In response, I hardened and compartmentalized my heart still more, driving me to risky and attention-grabbing behavior that could have—and except for God's sovereignty, should have—cost me my life.

Dad was a survivor. He grew up in not one but two addictive and abusive homes. Rather than nurture the children, his parents focused on social responsibilities, drinking, and providing material comforts. After a difficult divorce, Dad's mother remarried into an even more socially focused, business-driven, alcoholic, and abusive relationship. Dad and his two siblings were relegated to an area in the third-floor attic so as to be out of sight and mind from the home's patriarch.

The cruelty and violence of the family eventually sent Dad's sister to an insane asylum and drove his brother to commit suicide after four failed marriages. Dad survived, and even flourished in many ways. Yet his wounded and tattered heart actively avoided every emotionally charged issue. Perhaps he tried, but as a child, I can't remember Dad ever intervening on my behalf as my heart was being daily pillaged. I never experienced Dad as a, or my, *defender*, even when Mom's pathologies seemed to be destroying me. Dad cared for us in the only way he knew how—financially, which certainly comes with benefits, but he severely neglected the spiritual, emotional nurture children need from dads.

I now know Dad didn't do anything because he was cruel, but rather because he too was wounded. He brought into our lives a gregarious sense of humor, likely honed to mask his pain. This was a blessing, but a child's heart needs so much more.

In an attempt to survive the threefold hammering of my heart, at a very early age, I learned two survival behaviors deep down inside: *hiding* and *hardening*. I hid from the spiritual, emotional, and psychological harm and hardened against anything remotely good for me. As I hid in the creek near my childhood home, I broke rocks, built dams, and conversed with many imaginary friends.

## TAKE HEART

One miraculous day, I broke a flinty-hard red heart-shaped rock in half and discovered a freestanding window-cross shape inside—the same rock pictured above that I've kept for the fifty-three years since! Little did I know at the time that God would transform the *window* into my childhood stony-hard heart into a *cross* twenty-three years later at my conversion at age thirty-three.

I now know my parents did the best they could, given the examples of their own highly imperfect homes, the woundedness of their own hearts, and the deep limitations their wounds created. My parents had wonderful traits that endeared them to others and me. I'm blessed to have forgiven much and loved them much, now that I have spent many years sorting through memories and teasing out truths from falsehoods of my experiences and the always-very-complicated impact on my heart, spirit, and life.

Spending three years in intensive counseling after my conversion as a Christian contributed greatly to knowing my story and allowing God—via a trusted counselor and the Bible—to apply "holy forgetfulness" and redeem it each painful, yet redemptive, step of the way (Phil. 3:13-14). As we will see, "teasing out the truths and falsehoods" is an integral part of God's protocol for redemptive suffering.

As I have said, and will likely say again: what is most personal is most universal. I go into these details about my background because my story is so "uniquely common."

Perhaps you can empathize with parts of my story, even as you ponder your own.

More and more children today grow up in homes that are spiritually and emotionally abusive, which is the beginning of a cascade of problems that manifest them themselves in psychological- mental and physical maladies. (Please note the order matters here: (1) spiritual ailments beget 2) emotional ambivalence/infirmities, which propagate (3) psychological-mental disorders, which manifest themselves in (4) physical afflictions of all sorts and levels on the spectrum.)

So how and where does God say we need to begin to solve any problem of any sort? Yes, at the level of our spirituality and according to his design and plan of rescue, reconciliation, and redemption (John 3:16).

Children are hurt, both by what the adults around them do and by what they fail to do. Just like my story, more children than ever live in homes infected with rampant and increasingly pathological narcissism. Maybe you are among those who are forced to live out a parent's dream of often-unattainable athletic success or career achievement or winning beauty pageants or racking up AP classes. Other children find themselves ignored, emotionally abandoned, or treated as an inconvenience. Still, others live out a whirlwind of unending activities, ever distracted, always anonymous in their own homes, never able to know or grow comfortable with their own identity from God.

The picture preceding [page 79] is of a flinty hard stone I found at age ten. It was broken in half, and the break revealed a freestanding window (as I called it early in life). It is the perfect symbol of God's comfort upon finding this stone as a little boy as well as the reality of my heart twenty years later, when the window would be transformed into a cross upon my conversion. It becomes more obvious to me each and every day that I have been comforted so that in some way, shape, or form I can offer God's comfort to others (2 Cor. 1:3–7). Such comfort is real, as we are about to see, even in the deepest of tragedies.

Again, if it's not obvious by now it's worth repeating: I fell to my knees next to my mortally wounded father on Christmas night at an exact time and particular part of *my* story. I brought all of the untold sins and brokenness to bear as well as all of the redemptive glory God had wrought in my heart up until that moment. I cried out to God in that place some 20 years *following* my conversion. And the Spirit answered in such a personal way that it had universal application! This in my story and yours as well, Beloved.

## Out of Nowhere Heartbreak Can Happen

The spotlight in the garden that night seemed to be the only light in the entire world. As I fell to my knees next to my father, the cold seemed to disappear. Noises from the street, even the approaching sirens, sounded oddly muffled. As if in slow motion, I fell to my knees, sobbing. "Oh, Dad. Oh, Dad. Oh, Dad."

With each successive cry, I felt myself plummeting deeper and deeper. I was falling…and falling…and falling. Downward I fell with an ever-increasing sense of panic, a sense my free fall might never stop. With each successive "Oh, Dad!" I felt more out of control. I rocked, fell, and wept. Nearly nauseous, I looked around me, desperate to find something solid on which to steady myself. I looked down—and saw Dad's favorite .9mm pistol lying next to him, under his right hip in the snow where he had fallen. Then I saw the blood pooled under his head.

That's when I noticed Dad was still alive. He was shivering occasionally, barely breathing, and I had the distinct sense he was both here yet not here anymore. Although the first aid and rescue experience I had gained from many years living in the Colorado Rockies told me to stabilize him, I somehow knew nothing I could do would help or bring him back. I simply and absolutely wanted only to be there.

I knew I was meant to be exactly where I was. To kneel next to my dad in the snow. To pray to God. To weep. To seek. To plead. To speak and to listen, until that moment when the rest of the world would come crashing in upon the disastrous and dark yet sacred bubble of timelessness and space I had entered. Somehow, somewhere in the deepest recesses of my heart, I knew this was a unique moment I would never again have this time with Dad and God.

I rocked and wept uncontrollably, desperately grasping to maintain some connectedness to reality. As I wept, I fell and fell and fell ever deeper into my own personal, and yet very public, abyss of pain. It was personal, because I sensed Dad's loneliness and determination, my own guilt, regretting the things I could have or should have done or said but had not, and the searing pain that so many others close to Dad would feel very soon. It was public, because I saw in stark relief all humankind's desolation, self-isolation, and broken-heartedness.

Clearly, part of my own heart often said, "I do not need God's or anyone else's charity." I could imagine how the backed-into-a-corner "necessity" of suicide had overtaken my dad, as I considered how it had captured parts of my own heart at times. The darkness grew more real than I could have previously imagined. Then just as I felt I would completely lose myself in despair, I squeezed out a small cry from the very center of my heart: "Lord Jesus, please help me in this. Please help, Lord. Please."

It was then I noticed that each barely audible cry of "Oh, Dad," "Oh, God, please," I began to be enveloped by a unique and specific "response." Yes. That's what I would call it, a response. It came from within me yet from outside me.

At first, out of fear, I tried to push the words away. I had to stand up, to silence the words. I walked back to the glassed-in porch to gather whatever blankets I could find. Then I knelt next to Dad again, covered him, and protected him as best I could against the winter's night. It felt like pitifully too little, too late.

"Oh, Dad. Oh, God."

As I repeated the tearful refrain, the responses began again, this time more clearly—a series of verses from scripture, two verses the Bible and the Holy Spirit had given to me at specific times over the past fifteen years and one I wasn't as familiar with:

> *In the beginning...God said...*
> *(Gen. 1:1)*

> *In the beginning was the Word...*
> *(John 1:1)*

> *Be strong and courageous. Do not fear or be in dread...for it is the LORD your God who goes with you. He will never leave you or forsake you.*
> *(Deut. 31:6)*

Commanding yet quiet. Sweet. Scary. Soothing. Distinct, yet somehow elusive. The words began to attach me to an entirely new reality in that present moment. They formed the perfect answer for my pain. Yes, the words, the truths were the perfect answer for my pain. I shuddered deeply and sucked in my breath, wiping the pooling tears and phlegm from my face.

The words of each passage began distinctly, overlapped, and then melted away into the night. The circle of sounds and words then repeated itself, distinct yet still, quiet and overlapping. Oh, how I had loved these passages, these promises, well before this dark night of the soul! Nevertheless, I could not have imagined how perfectly they fit together and how tightly I would hold on to them in this moment of deep weeping as I peered into the window of my own heart. I could never have anticipated this context and the far-deeper meaning and sweet solace they would bring both to me and eventually to the many others crushed by Dad's suicide.

## The Free Fall and Foundations of Christmas Night

Suddenly, I realized my rocking had slowed. I painfully straightened my back and glanced around. I checked Dad's condition. It was the same. The sirens still wailed in the distance, strangely muffled yet timelessly imminent. My free fall had ceased. Without knowing when, I had somehow landed on something as firm and solid as I could ever imagine. Thousands of words, hundreds of attempts to describe what happened would never fully explain the experience.

I had landed. I knew it. I knew I could never go lower or sink deeper because I was resting fully on God, on the Rock. The only true God, who had spoken *creation* into existence, would never leave me. The *Word* who was there "in the beginning," the Savior of the world, the God of those magnificent "beginnings" held even Dad's choice within his perfect and providential purpose. I knew, without being able to explain it, God's plan was perfect and rooted to something solid, deep, and abiding. I had no idea what would happen after this moment, nor did I need to know. I could trust God for the future because I was kneeling, resting on something as solid and immovable as the eternal Rock himself that consisted of his mighty acts of *creation*, of incarnating *Christ*, and of a promise of never-ending *covenant* love. Creation, Christ, and Covenant—a three-pillared foundation connected to the ends of the universe.

Significantly, this first group of Bible passages from God ended with his promise to abide with me and intimately comfort me, to keep on caring for me with his promise never to leave me or to forsake me ever. His love, just for me, buoyed me up, brought confidence and hope in a way nothing else could have. And although I didn't realize it at the time, God was perfectly and especially there for my dad as well. This Christmas night, I grasped afresh how unspeakably vast God is yet how very personally he cares for me. I saw for the first time the full glory and greatness of God—God who was there just for me, God who is always there for every heart that turns to him in times of weeping or free fall.

This night of weeping and kneeling happened twenty years after my conversion and forms the centerpiece of how God blessed me (and can bless you) that night. The order and timing of those exact scriptures fashioned the perfect response to exactly what I needed from the Spirit in that moment. In the first set of passages provided me by the Spirit, I knew the first two passages well, but the third I didn't; I would have never placed them in the perfect order that God the Spirit did. Coming passages have the same miracle in common, and it blows my mind to this day. Admittedly, I am one who pays a great deal of attention to the grand and granular stuff of life, a mixed blessing in many ways.

## TAKE HEART

Choking back tears and uncontrollable groans, I was able to trace how God had begun by reminding me of creation first. This calmed and eased my breathing. I could remember how God had started and sustained everything, everything, everything from the core of my heart to the farthest reaches of the universe. God the Father thought, God the Son spoke, and God the Spirit hovered-fluttered, and all creation leapt into existence; and God sustained every atom, including this very evening I knelt with Dad on Christmas night.

All creation "thought, uttered, and fluttered" into existence by God the Father, Son, and Spirit? Yes! Oh yes, it was and is true. What an awesome creating and sustaining God he is. Could God then be trusted to remember Dad and me in the garden even now, even here? Yes! Why had this reminder—that the Trinity shared in creating the universe—been the first pillar in the foundation? In God's mercy, grandness, and attentiveness to my deepest pain, he began in the beginning, the assurance that he created it all and most carefully sustains it all—every detail, providentially and perfectly.

It was as if God was reminding me, "John, John. I hear your pain. I feel your deepest despair. I know your intense fear of free-falling into the shock and darkness of this tragedy. You were never formed by me to experience this sort of free fall. No one is. It's not in your true nature as it was 'in the beginning.' But remember, remember. I began it all, and I am in and through it all today…until I bring it all to its consummation. It's foundational: I am Creator and Sustainer."

Then the second verse and truth began to overlap and ascend into and through my heart for attention: "In the beginning was the Word…" (John 1:1). While kneeling in this sacred time and place, this incredibly rich "second beginning", referring to none other than Jesus Christ himself, carried with it an even greater measure of remembrance, meaning, intimacy, and gratitude than I could ever fully describe. God led me from Creator to Creator Incarnate. No more appropriate gift could have followed the first reminder of God creating creation to Jesus, born, died, and resurrected for me.

This remembrance of Christ's beginnings as the Word incarnate come to "dwell among us" echoed back from my outcry could not have been a more perfect next step for God to reach into my heart and stop the free fall. Graciously, there was more, a third passage: loving words from God to not be afraid, to have courage, and that he would never leave me or forsake me.

Again it was as though God had said, "John, dear one, remember I spoke it all in the beginning for my pleasure and your blessing; I sent my Son to redeem it when all went wrong. Surely, beloved, you can trust that I am not only aware of your deep hurt, but I am with you now and always will be, as we move through this together. I began it all. I am sustaining and redeeming it all. I'm with you for all time and eternity, beloved."

These foundational promises moved down to the final level of assurance and friendship in "I will never leave you…Never ever, ever, ever… No way, no how. No matter what sort of free fall of any kind, I will always be with you, John. Get out your faith. Use it now. Do you trust me in this? I can and will bless you and others. I will never leave you or forsake you no matter what may come. Yes, and lots more will come. But in it all, in it all, I am always with you, John."

This foundation I now knelt upon was so unshakable it included every aspect of the universe, including Dad and I in the garden and including you this very minute. Anything else that might ever occur in my life that might throw me back into a state of dark meaninglessness, existential vertigo, and hopelessness of any kind can never, ever undo or shake apart this unshakable foundation that I now rested upon.

## A Reminder: The Primacy of Free Falls and Foundations

Please recall the two very effective illustrations on pp 76-77. At this point, we must absolutely pause to take into account this part of God's protocol for redemptive suffering: free falls and foundations. This was so huge. Why? Because when building anything in life, we must have full assurance of the integrity of the foundation. If you were to move on too quickly from establishing the foundations, it would detract significantly from the other parts of God's protocol for redemptive suffering, which we will be talking about.

So let's think together about the important implications of all foundations, and your foundation. As Image Bearers of

God, every human being is created to flourish with God as the foundation of their life, which will result in either a radically blessed or a blasphemous and despairing life (when choosing other foundations). Please consider free falls and foundations more personally:

- All weeping, tears, trials, and free falls from living in a broken world are God's merciful offer for revealing, modifying, and firming up the foundations of your life.
- In a broken world, spiritual, emotional, psychological, or physical free falls occur every day. It's not a matter of *if* but when.
- Regardless of our level of suffering, God desires we go back to be reminded and rerooted deeper and deeper into the foundations of Creation, Christ, and Covenant.
- Every human being, Christian or not, has faith in something—something that acts as a foundation for their life. Trials test the nature and worthiness of everyone's faith foundations.
- If the foundation of your faith is not God's Creation, Jesus Christ, and his Covenant promises, then trials—little and big free falls of any kind—will harden your heart, make you bitter rather than better, and estrange you more from God and others.
- Please slow down, have patience, be honest, and take some time to look more closely than ever at the foundations of your life. Are they the pillars of Creation, Christ, and Covenant?

## *TAKE HEART*

- Perhaps, without even knowing it, the foundations of your identity and life are more about your work, material possessions, looks, social status, victimhood, need to be in control, role as an exemplary parent, popularity, intellect, successes, athletic prowess, being the life of the party, unworthiness, or family history. Is anything other than God's Creation, Christ, and Covenant acting as the foundation(s) for your life?
- If so, they cannot sustain the weight of the glory of who you are purely as an image bearer of God, let alone who you are in Christ. Not one of these "faulty and frail foundations" can withstand the freefalls of life. Or—please get this—if they apparently can withstand life's trials, this is what these idols will do: enslave you by demanding more of you than God does without any of the mercies God employs when you can't make it. As I said earlier, having no faith in God only results in having a lot of faith in lesser gods or things that will come crashing down, leave, or forsake you all day long, over and over again, until anger and despair are your only food and drink.
- But all of life's most radical ups and downs are not simply to be handled and healed by God; rather, they can be redeemed in ways that are unimaginable—if we're resting on the foundations.
- Whether we know or admit it, attempting to live life devoid of God's foundations of Creation, Christ, and Covenant will force us to hide, harden, and be full of the anxieties of yesterday, fears of

today, and worries of tomorrow—and that's no way to live life. I (and many others) have tried.
- Lastly—albeit there's always more—living a faithful, maturing, and increasingly effective Christ-centered life is based upon not only resting and relying on the foundation of the Bible's Creation, Christ, and Covenant, but also by deepening and growing more and more in our faith based upon these three pillars and pilings of the faith: the *foundations* for our life serve as a *platform* for life as well!
- In reality, there is absolutely no way of exhausting the breadth and depth of what God has in store for those of us who will grow deep roots down into the foundations or "soil" of Creation, Christ, and Covenant: Please begin, shore up, and deepen your faith beginning "today" (Ps. 95:7–8).

# 6

# The Window:
# Fallen, Forgiven, Free

**Applying Romans 1:18 and Romans 8:1**

**STEP 2. ONCE ON A FOUNDATION OF CREATION, CHRIST, AND COVENANT, WE ARE ASSURED NO PUNISHMENT IS INVOLVED, ONLY PURIFICATION: SEARCHING OUR HEART, DISCERNING BETWEEN THE FALSEHOODS AND TRUTHS OF OUR FAITH.**

## JOHN O. DOZIER, JR.

*The Would-a, Could-a, Should-a's: All trials of any kind are accompanied by "waves of true and false guilt" that can either be identified and redeemed to offer God the glory and a blessing to us, or disregarded, and offer glory to self—and result in a hardened and embittered heart.*

## TAKE HEART

*The Window: All weeping, wounds open a window into our heart so that we can more clearly see our hearts as God does. We must spend time with The Holy Spirit, a community of faith, and wise counsel so that we can tease apart the truths and falsehoods of our heart—then sanctification, maturity, holiness can occur, and we become more like Jesus Christ in and through our trials.*

While in this place of timelessness with Dad, God reminded me he used the same approach with his hurting or wandering ones in the Bible. He asked Job where he was when it all began in *creation*. Paul and other inspired writers began nearly every letter to the suffering church by reminding them of who they were in *Christ*, not in the world. Old and New Testament writers referred again and again to God's promise, commitment, and unswerving love of his beloved in *covenant*—even the promise to sacrifice himself for us.

Now I knew the faith I had often held abstractly had become reality. The change to my subjective experience and internalization of my faith was beyond anything I ever experienced. My powerful Creator-God and his Son, Jesus, were the rock-solid foundation of the universe, and I was resting on it, making never-ending sinking or falling an absolute impossibility.

For the time being, I knew better than ever that God's beginnings in creation and Christ and his promise to never forsake me would make it possible for me to take my next step—and the step after that, ad infinitum. As I regained my composure for just that moment, I saw in my deep and painful weeping that a window within my heart had been opened. Through that open window into my heart, I would soon see important connections between the past, present, and future. Through that window, I would see how God would use even this horror for his glory and for the good of many people. First through the *weeping* then the *window*, I would eventually see the *way* so much closer to God and to those around me.

I wanted to pause, to stay in this bubble of God's protective care forever. Yet I knew I could not. The crush of the world's response to my dad's suicide as well as the crush of another sort lay just around the corner.

> *I am feeble and utterly crushed; I groan in anguish of heart.*
> *(Ps. 38:8)*

> *You hurled me into the deep, into the very heart of the seas, and the currents swirled about me; all your waves and breakers swept over me.*
> *(Jon. 2:3)*

The bubble of God's timelessness and protective care held me in place on my knees next to Dad as the sirens wailed ever closer in the distance. The promises of God's creative power and personal presence had placed a foundation beneath me. I landed and would fall no further.

Slowly, I straightened my back to breathe, clear my head, and check my surroundings. My body ached with the stress of coursing emotions. It felt as if I had been straining and ripping apart every muscle in my body for weeks. Tears still welled in my eyes as I leaned back, then forward to place my hands on Dad's side and shoulder.

## All Weeping Opens (Cracks, Pries, Blasts) a Window into Your Heart

By now, the pain of everything that had happened—the weeping—had flung the window of my heart open wide. Through that window, I could see previously hidden parts of myself more clearly than ever before, especially as I considered my relationship with my dad. Certainly in such a time feelings of *false guilt* will likely arise, and they did. Far more troubling, though, were the sights of *true guilt*, and self-centeredness and sin within my heart as the window into my heart was blown open wide.

## The Pain and the Blessing of Looking In

Once secured on the foundations of the faith, I was free to see the truth of my guilt for my father's lack of faith, his fatal shooting, his sense of aloneness and futility, and the innumerable ways I failed in my relationship with him. Now it was too late. Wave after wave of *would-a, could-a, should-a's*—a deadly mixture of true and false guilt—began to wash and crush over me.

The Spirit had used this time of weeping to fling wide the window of my heart to reveal my sin in such an overpowering way I could no longer deny it or paper over its seriousness. It ripped my heart into pieces, but we worship a God who only rips in order to mend. I understood the depth of David's pain as he pleaded, "Against you, you only, have I sinned and done what is evil in your sight; so you are right in your verdict and justified when you judge" (Ps. 51:4). God had brought me to a second blessed cry of the heart.

"Father God," I prayed. "Please, forgive me. Please forgive my silence. Forgive my pride, my will for control, my neediness, and my slavery to the opinions of others. Forgive me for presuming upon your mercies, for just assuming you would always give me another day to muster up my courage, to tell my story—the story of sin and of your Son's cross, the story I never shared with the consistency and courage I could have with Dad. Forgive me for living not out of your power but my own. Please forgive my sins of omission and commission. Forgive me especially for the hypocrisy that you abhor, Lord. Please forgive it all. Please, Lord. Before I'm utterly crushed, please."

As I fell suddenly silent, a response to my cries began to form. Just as before, the words came from within me, yet from outside me as well. The words I heard in my heart were passages and promises I had studied before. Yet now my heart embraced them, grasping the truth as never before. The answer to my cries was opening before me, with the toughest, sweetest, most delicious words possible:

**The wrath of God is being revealed from heaven against all the godlessness and wickedness of men who suppress the truth.**
**(Rom. 1:18)**

**Therefore, there is now no condemnation for those who are in Christ Jesus.**
**(Rom. 8:1)**

A shivering-stuttering-hiccup-and-sobbing chill ran throughout my entire body as I took in the truth of my sinful condition and the promise of God's incredible forgiving love. "Suppressing the truth…in wickedness"—I had done that many times in my relationship with my father! These words cut to the heart of my heart to reveal the dark truth that my fears, shame, control, and pride had prevented me from "speaking the truth in love." These things had kept me from sharing with my own dad, and with many others, my spiritual journey.

As that truth cut through me, threatening to separate sinew from bone, another truth flowed over me as well: "There is now no condemnation." Now, nothing—nothing—could separate me from the love of God. By means of the sacrificial death of Jesus Christ, God has taken away all my sin!

These passages—perhaps two of the most powerful and reassuring promises in the entire Bible—drifted across my mind and heart, blessing me with peace beyond comprehension. I could almost taste the truth of the Gospel message as it had been summarized by my most influential spiritual mentor, Tim Keller: "You are more sinful than you could ever imagine, yet you are more loved than you ever dared hope for." There it was, so starkly plain and laid out before me: a perfect encapsulation of the gospel!

It's true, I thought. But now, now I knew it to be true on an *entirely* different level than ever before. I went from knowing the truth to palpably tasting, feeling, and loving the truth. My heart had melted as I—though in a fresh, renewed way—thought about my sin and about the promise in Christ of no condemnation...no condemnation or shame at all.

I had spoken, written, warned, counseled, and consoled others again and again about how God will providentially and powerfully use the circumstances of this broken world to bring people back to himself—first, if they do not already believe and have faith in Jesus; or, second, closer to him if they already did have a relationship with him. That's God's plan of redemption: offering salvation, maturing by sanctification—all for serving others in Jesus's name! There's no limit on the times we benefit from hearing, "Saved and sanctified to serve."

I had meditated often on his promise of revealing and removing idols hidden in our heart in order to "break and remove our heart of stone and, purely by his mercy, give us a heart of flesh" first in *conversion* (e.g., Ezek. 11; 36; John 3:3; 2 Cor. 5:17) and then in sanctification (e.g., John 17; Rom. 6:5–6; 2 Cor. 4:7–18; James 1:1).

But this? On Christmas night? To my dad? To me? And to so many others in our lives who would be blasted and possibly broken—but may be blessed—by the shock and the loss? I did not yet fully know how to answer the questions flying through my heart and spirit. But I did know one thing with more confidence than I could ever have imagined knowing anything: *it's true*. What was that it? Simply and beautifully this:

**For God so loved the world (he so loves me), that he gave his one and only Son, that whoever believes in him shall not perish but have eternal life. (John 3:16, parentheses added)**

The assurance of being on a firm foundation while being at a window peering into my heart was extremely real. I was, at last, being real; I was more sinful yet more loved. This is the Gospel. In me. And I hope in you. Do not ever walk away from the opened window of your heart.

Now on the foundations of Creation, Christ, and Covenant, I knew stopping and looking into the window of my heart was not for *punishment* but *purification*. This distinction couldn't be more important for you and me to grasp and hold on to as tight as could be: we are freed to be real about our saved-but-still-sin-filled hearts. The good news is that this is what Jesus came to do.

## Hearts in the Fiery Furnace to be Transformed and Set Free

Scripture clearly describes Christ's deep and compassionate care for our hearts. After all, his entire life was filled with the agony of anticipation of the price he would pay on the cross to redeem Adam's choice and children—you and me—who have horribly misused their hearts. It's important to note that the title of this booklet, Take Heart, expresses Jesus's desire for our hearts: "Above all else, guard your heart, for it is the wellspring of life" (Prov. 4:23).

Imagine Jesus sitting with you, looking into the window of your heart, reminding you his purpose in suffering for the non-Christian is to help us have a change of heart about God and our need for a Savior. For the Christian, he wants to further transform our converted, born-again, new heart into the likeness of Jesus. This is God's plan of redemption: change the hearts of the faithless and conform the hearts of the faithful—until Jesus returns to make all things new. Where is your heart on what we have covered thus far?

In much of his teaching, Jesus confronted the crises created by divided hearts—hearts compartmentalized and focused on good things made only things by the idol factory known as the human heart. Listen to Jesus lament our divided heart: "You hypocrites! Well did Isaiah prophesy of you, when he said: 'This people honors me with their lips, but their heart is far from me; in vain do they worship me, teaching as doctrines the commandments of men'" (Matt. 15:7–9).

In contrast, Jesus continually called attention to his intention for our hearts. Consider one example:

*One of the scribes came up and...asked him, "Which commandment is the most important of all?" Jesus answered, "The most important is, 'Hear, O Israel: The Lord our God, the Lord is one. And you shall love the Lord your God with all your heart and with all your soul and with all your mind and with all your strength.'"*
*(Mark 12:28–30)*

But Jesus's ministry went well beyond mere warnings and instruction. Please get this: the Son of God willingly left glory, came to Earth as a vulnerable infant, lived as a man of sorrows, was despised, was rejected, sacrificed himself upon the cross, suffered the undeserved condemnation and silence of his own Father—all to make it possible to fulfill God's promise to save and change the hearts of all who believe:

***I will give them one heart, and a new spirit I will put within them. I will remove the heart of stone from their flesh and give them a heart of flesh.***
***(Ezek.11:19)***

***For God so loved the world, that he gave his only Son, that whoever believes in him should not perish but have eternal life.***
***(John 3:16)***

***Therefore, if anyone is in Christ, he is a new creation. The old has passed away; behold, the new has come.***
***(2 Cor. 5:17)***

***And he who was seated on the throne said, "Behold, I am making all things new." Also he said, "Write this down, for these words are trustworthy and true."***
***(Rev.21:5)***

Jesus Christ, by the person of the Spirit, is most merciful, all-powerful, and transformational as he stands with us at the windows of our hearts during the unavoidable bumps, bruises, and bludgeoning we experience, helping us see the purposes of redemption—not just healing, not just self-help, not just assuaging pain, not just getting you and me back to a place of comfort but real, redeemed, and resurrection of life! This is what *better* means: for the Christian, becoming more and more like Christ.

## TAKE HEART

In what specific ways might you (with another's help, perhaps) search your own heart for falsehoods or feelings of any heart-hardening, unnecessary, or unhealthy condemnation? Or perhaps there exists realms of true and worthy guilt that need to be revealed, aired, confessed, and redeemed as well? Stay put, be real, and feel secure in Christ while at the window of your heart. It's time well worth your while spending.

## The Paraclete* and Peering In

*one who consoles, one who intercedes on our behalf, a comforter or an advocate (Name for the Holy Spirit)*

A long while back—like it was yesterday—during a particularly dark and difficult trial in my life, I reached out via e-mail to numerous brothers in Christ for prayers in a time of deep weeping. One pal, John Berry, sent the simplest yet most robust and profound response. It was a Spirit-led reflection of the fact that he got it—he had been matured and made wise by suffering, and he wanted to pass along the difficult yet massively blessed modus operandi. John wrote, "Stay put."

When it comes to more and more fully recouping and redeeming and then passing along the Christ-likeness included in any and all suffering God allows in our life, "staying put" has a time and place that is *absolutely* crucial. We have too much to listen for, too much to be more God- and self-aware of, too much to learn, too much to taste, too much to mature, too much to become more holy, too much to be transformed and conformed, and too much to bless others with *not* to do so!

On the positive side, staying put acknowledges the investment required of any and all our time, talent, and treasure to take full advantage of the trials God's sovereignty orchestrates in the divine symphony of our life. On the negative side, staying put is being brutally yet lovingly honest about the fact that the very first thing most of us do when suffering occurs is to consciously and unconsciously look to flee. To move on as fast as we can; get distracted ASAP; keep things on the surface; deny the emotional or psychological pain, ambivalence of any sort; anesthetize ourselves in a host of ways; get back to life, work, busyness, even helping others before we help ourselves—all to avoid the "redemptive introspection" God so much desires: part and parcel of transforming the heart, spirit and will to be more like Jesus.

Jesus's person and power is made manifest through the Spirit, whose presence I felt keenly that night, offering me a place alongside him as we peered through the window of my heart. Being with the Holy Spirit to look into my heart is no small matter and an unspeakable gift offered to me and all who would, by faith, to stay put for a time.

When you experience suffering, remember the same unspeakable gift is being offered to you. Stay put. Abide for as long as it takes. God's redeeming love and truth heals and then uses the hurt to holistically transform and turn our lives around so that the very pain is the point of beauty, whereby our commitment and compassion to live like

## *TAKE HEART*

Jesus is spread abroad in the world. Stay put. Do not let the world's, your own fallenness and fears, or the devil's temptations to avoid discomfort make you flee this precious and temporally and eternally profitable time at the blown open window of your heart—the center of your being.

Seeing the two sides of my true nature through the window into my heart (being more sinful yet more loved) was a view of reality that would have been impossible to fully accept if it weren't for two main facts: first, that I was on the foundation of the Creation, Christ, and Covenant promise; and second, being very, very close to the person of the Holy Spirit in a sacred place. There was a deep sense that I should take full advantage of this rare and rich time to be with the loving guide, counselor, and pointer to Jesus Christ: the Holy Spirit (and in the months following, with a trusted counselor).

It's important to note again that no other circumstance of life would avail me to this searing yet sacred experience of seeing the truth and embracing it so that I could (with the help of the Helper, the Bible, and my Christian community) eradicate the lies and live more and more according to who I really, truly am in Jesus Christ. Nobody volunteers for radical surgery, let alone heart surgery. But spiritually speaking, it's what our hearts need every day: to eradicate falsehoods and fill the void with truth, cutting away the stony places and grafting in flesh (Ezek. 11:19; 36:26; 2 Tim. 2:21; John 17:17).

Heartbreak is God's offer for an increase of our wholehearted love and devotion to God and neighbor. And this is no small thing—if embraced, this can transform a heart and the world; if avoided, this can and does propagate bitterness, despair, and isolation in a host of ways.

Despite fear and even a desire to flee what I might see, I was overwhelmed by an opportunity to see my heart as God sees it and to experience his pure love for me, his longing for my purification and the eventual holiness of my heart. Like Paul, I had the rare chance to distinguish between the "I, as sinner" and the "I, as saved" (Rom. 7) as I peered through the window into the recesses of my heart.

## We Have to Spend the Time to Take Care of Our Hearts

### *Teach me your way, O LORD, that I may walk in your truth; unite my heart to fear your name. (Ps. 86:11)*

*Resolved, after afflictions, to inquire, what I am the better for them, and what good I have got by them.*
*(Jonathan Edwards)*

*A true faith in Jesus Christ will not suffer us to be idle. No, it is an active, lively, restless principle; it fills the heart, so that it cannot be easy till it is doing something for Jesus Christ.*
*(George Whitefield, preacher in the Church of England, 1714–1770)*

## TAKE HEART

Time spent at the window of our heart blown open by life's many travails is both a trial and a treasure. Think about it. Have you experienced this truism? Have you had a keener, more mature, and more realistic assessment of your heart (e.g., what you put your trust in, your core beliefs, non-negotiables, dreams, hopes, etc.) about life in or after heartbreak of some kind? The treasure far exceeds the trial, but the trial must occur to promote the kind of heart change offered as my heart was crushed and recreated by the Holy Spirit. God opens the window to the heart; we must faithfully look inside and see, and not do it alone.

The theology of being at the window and seeing "the two sides of the Gospel"—more sinful yet more loved—more clearly than ever gave me glimpses of how important and necessary the time at the window truly was. In fact, God tells us that even the angels long to look into the Gospel this way (1 Pet. 1:12). Why? Because, as we've seen and will see again, the heart of the matter is a matter of the heart. Utterly surrounded by God the Father's, God the Son's, and Holy Spirit's mercy, I must stay in this place where Jesus's words faintly echoed, "I did not come to bring peace, but a sword...to divide...truth from falsehood...beginning in the heart" (Matt. 10:34, paraphrased).

## Don't Waste the Cutting in the Curse of Suffering

The "stay-putness" I felt as the Holy Spirit assured me my specific outcries tied to the true and false guilt would be answered was palpable. In this place with God and Dad, I had seen the monumental gulf between (a) "The wrath of God…being revealed…against all…who suppress the truth" and (b) the blessed, gracious promise that now there is "no condemnation for those who are in Christ Jesus."

The nearly unbelievable assurance of "no condemnation" had swept away every one of my would-a, could-a, should-a's, giving me the freedom to choose life or death, darkness or light, self or Christ, idols or the living God. No promise from God has ever taken a higher hill in life's battle than had this promise: "It's true."

I wept, even as I knelt over Dad's body in the Christmas snow, bittersweet tears in experiencing the Gospel that I was a sinner saved by grace, more aware of my sin contrasted with God's love in Christ than ever before.

I suddenly became more aware of what was going on around me. The now-imminent sounds of the world responding to an emergency began to break into my protective bubble. Once again, I checked Dad's condition. Once again, it was unchanged. His body continued to shiver, his breathing becoming ever more shallow and erratic.

## Count the Blessings of Better Knowing Your Heart

The following is a quote from Harold Simonson about Jonathan Edwards's commitment to the subject I'm driving home here: "the relentless need to distinguish between the true and false affections." This most worthy, God-honoring, and people-blessing objective is never more apropos and available to us than when the storms of life blow the window of our heart off its hinges. Stay put for a while.

*No secrets of the heart and mind remained hidden when Jonathan Edwards called for self-scrutiny, this meant the relentless need to distinguish between the true and false affections; between those affections having to do with a redeemed heart, and those darkened by sin. To clarify these distinctions was Edwards' purpose in his life and in seeing the Great Awakening come to pass.*
*(Harold Simonson)*

To summarize and take hold of God's protocol:

1) Once on a foundation of Creation, Christ, and Covenant, the Christian is assured no punishment is involved in our trials, only purification. In Christ, our punishment was fully taken care of on the cross (Mark 16:16; Rom. 8; 10:9; Eph. 1).

2) Suffering is a one-of-a-kind opportunity to partner with the Spirit (and the Christian community) to transform our hearts of stone into hearts of flesh into the likeness of Jesus's heart. It's a journey that takes time; do not underestimate the importance of this change of heart. As you can see, it's a "cathartically purging partnership" between the Spirit's *supernatural* work/dynamism and *your own* trust in God, obedience, staying put and cooperation.

3) The inevitable trials of life vary in the duration and depth of pain. Each should be understood at a level of detail where true and lasting transformation can

take place before we try and "move on" or "get back to life."

4) Imagine a window of your heart being blown open by a trial in life. Explain what it might be like to "sit at the window of your heart" with the Lord. What might you see? How would the Holy Spirit console and counsel you?

5) Time, by itself, doesn't heal wounds; time intentionally and faithfully spent as God desires you spend it can and does! Spend some time—much more than you likely want to—biblically, wisely, trustingly, humbly, vulnerably, courageously, and in community: looking into sequestered and sealed-off realms of your heart. Get sound Christian counsel; be as real and honest with yourself as possible; don't be afraid to open all the well-sealed, even dark compartments within your heart. Did I say don't do this alone?

6) Purification and softening of the heart is at the centerpiece of God's plan of redemption; it's all about replacing falsehoods with God's truth and love and gaining God, self and other awareness. Devoid of this principle and process, our hearts will respond in the only way it can: to atrophy; to hide; to harden; to resent; and to become (more and more) self-centered, prideful, pretentious, fearful, worried, and alone. Without taking advantage of a window blown open into our heart by life's trials, we cannot hope to change at a deep level. Do you hope to change at a deep level?

## TAKE HEART

7) Only in the midst of our pain does a window fly open to reveal the content of our hearts. Due to the vestiges of sin, pride, shame, fear, condemnation, it doesn't stay open for long. You must, we must capitalize on this painful, yet unique, window of opportunity. Cleansing our hearts of falsehood and replacing the void with God's love and truth is at the centerpiece of the Trinity's plan to conform you into the likeness of Jesus Christ (Prov. 4:23; John 17:21; Rom. 8:28–29; 1 John 1:9). Avoiding this offer from God has dire consequences as well (Jer. 2; James 4:4; 1 John 2:15–17).

# 7

# The Way: Bringing Our Transformed Hearts Back into the Chaos

Applying Ezekiel 11:19; Romans 8:28, 12:2; and Job 19:25

**STEP 3: FOR THE "CO-REDEEMER IN CHRIST," THE WAY BACK INTO THE CHAOS OF A FALLEN AND BROKEN WORLD REQUIRES SUPERNATURAL AND HUMAN WILL POWER, PURPOSE, AND PREPARATION. DON'T WASTE YOUR TEARS.**

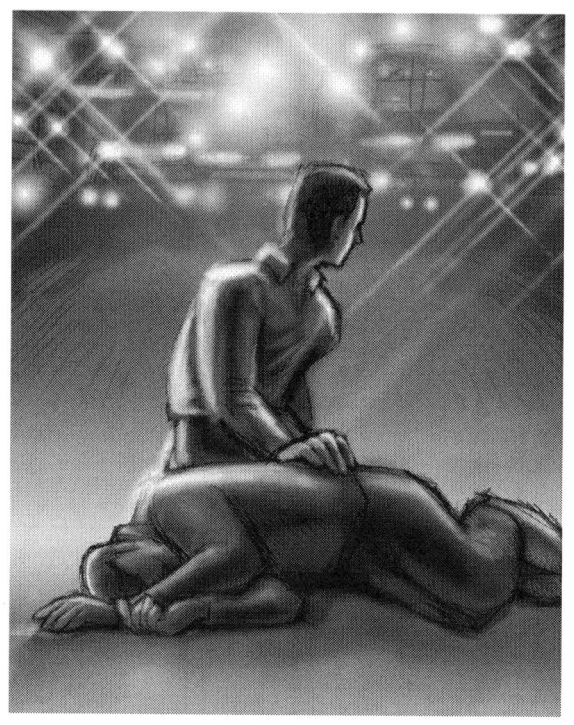

*Turned to Anticipate The Way: Anticipating, being wise and faithful, and planning how to return to a world of chaos and suffering is crucially important. Go deep, and do not rush the process.*

## TAKE HEART

*The Way of Moving Out into the Chaos: All of humanity, changed by suffering in some way, must turn and return to the world. Will we be more like Christ? Will we be bitter or better? The choice is ours to make.*

*JOHN O. DOZIER, JR.*

# Order Matters:
# Foundation First, Window Second

Foundations had been identified and secured. The window of God's truth and love—my sin and my security—had begun to help me differentiate between the true and false guilt. But the time had come to turn and face the wider chaos of this tragedy. *This was the proof in the pudding: would the restored foundations and a change of heart within me prevail over the abject brokenness I was about to face outside me?* I prayed, "Oh, God, do I hate the thought of turning to face this Hell on Earth. Please help me."

Time had lost all meaning, so I had no idea how much time had passed since I fell to my knees next to my father.

"Oh, Dad," I said for the last time as I rested my hands on his left side and shoulder.

How blessed I felt for the answers God had provided to my cries. For now, however, the world had begun to crash into my God-given bubble of the Spirit's timeless truth and love. Now it's time to purposefully move back into the chaos of this broken world, to be more like Jesus than I was before. This requires supernatural and human willpower, purpose, and preparation.

I tried to ease my stiff body as I continued kneeling next to Dad in the snow. Moving in a slow, surreal motion, I turned my head and shoulders to glance backward. My head pounded. My eyes burned. My body ached. As I turned, I noticed a new sensation. It seemed as though I had somehow partially reentered worldly real time, real space. The "bubble of protection" still existed, but it had changed as the outside world drew closer and began to intrude.

As the first of nearly a dozen emergency medical personnel and law enforcement officers approached, I could see lights flashing on the snow all around the neighborhood. Chaos threatened to encroach quickly into the place of calm, into the sacred space I had experienced with Dad and God.

As if from a surreal dream, taupe and blue-red forms came close. Bright yellow reflective bands on arms and legs. Black rubber, turned-down boots. Red, blue, and orange flashing lights. All suddenly seemed to swarm toward me. I blinked the crust and tears out of my eyes, wiping the mucus from my nose and mouth and trying to refocus on what was happening. But it was no use. I wasn't ready to leave this place, to leave my dad and being with God. Not yet.

I turned back to him for what seemed like a last good-bye. The anticipation of entering a whole new hell of chaos, consequences, and shattered hearts made me feel sick to my stomach.

"Breathe, John," I kept reminding myself.

I could already feel the crush of consolation and tears, the free falls, the shock and shame of suicide, the wailing and sympathy, the awkward immobility, the questions, and the stunned silence. I could already anticipate the many and painstaking steps needed to "deal with it all."

The inevitability that I would be the one to take charge of many of the details danced at the fringes of my mind. I lived in town. I was the only blood relative here. Somewhere deep within my mind and heart, I accepted that charge. I knew I would be ready, and in the recesses of my heart now shored up by God's comfort, I felt honored and deeply blessed by it. I knew people would come rushing in to help. I also knew God had been preparing me in so many ways for this exact time, for this exact moment and set of circumstances. I knew deep down inside my heart.

Still, I didn't want to leave the garden.

"Oh, God. Oh, God," my heart cried out.

I felt as if I had just finished a double marathon and now I had to stand up just as the starting gun exploded again, sending me off on the next one. My heart and emotions lay in shambles. Yet I was not lost by any means. Oh, no. I was resting on a rock-solid, firm foundation. I was reconciled to being fallen and forgiven. But I was not quite ready to step out of this sheltered place and into the shattering and shambles of many other broken hearts.

Then gradually, I began to realize I could breathe a lot better—physically, to be sure, but also emotionally, intellectually, and spiritually. Though I could not have articulated the impact of the conversations I had just had with God, I felt a deep sense of purpose, of promise, of peace. I had a heartfelt peace knowing everything would be better than OK. I was safe. I would not fall below the firm foundation God had set beneath me. I would never be more forgiven for what might have been or for what would be than I was at this precise moment. The Holy Spirit was very close, and he would bring many others to help me and those I loved get through this horrific tragedy.

I knew exactly what had happened and what was coming. It may not sound big that I knew what I knew. But this knowing was huge for me. It provided a deep sense of purpose, of peace, and it gave me the strength to take the next step no matter what would come in the next few hours, the next few days. The details didn't matter for now. I knew God would be there. I knew others would be there. I knew I was ready to respond. (I was at least partially correct.)

Then as I faced Dad and waited for the EMTs to cross the front lawn and take charge of the scene on this holy and most dreadful Christmas night, I heard new words circling my heart, words of prayer, of total dependence:

*Oh, God. I'm so blessed to have been here in this place, but what now, Lord? Please tell me, what now? I need your help to get through this, Lord. I cannot do it alone. Please, Lord, please give me the strength, the love, and the heart to move forward from here. Please hold me up, Lord. Please give me the hope, and show me the way to make it through this next horrible yet hopeful part.*

As I prayed, once again (and for the last time that night), the Spirit's blessed response to my heart's cry enfolded me. Passages from the Bible again came to me. Clear yet faint, bold yet quiet, overlapping yet discrete:

*I will give them one heart, and a new spirit I will put within them. I will remove the heart of stone from their flesh and give them a heart of flesh.*
*(Ezek.11:19)*

*We know that for those who love God all things work together for good, for those who are called according to his purpose.*
*(Rom. 8:28)*

*Do not be conformed to this world, but be transformed by the renewal of your mind, that by testing you may discern what is the will of God, what is good and acceptable and perfect.*
*(Rom. 12:2)*

*For I know that my Redeemer lives, and at the last he will stand upon the earth.*
*(Job 19:25)*

## An Extra Portion of God's Proof, Power, Provision, and Preparation

These proofs from God the Spirit's Scripture? These words of power? These truths of provision? These treasures to be prepared? Amazing!

I felt a deep shiver course through my body. It was as though God were giving me an extra measure, a second and third helping of his mercy. I took deep solace in each of these rich and redemptive passages.

## TAKE HEART

Then two contrasting emotions flooded my heart and began to overwhelm me: an inexplicably deep peace and a sickening foreboding. I coughed and shivered, breathing in the peace. The scripture passages quietly yet unequivocally coursed through me, deepening my peace with each breath, with each remembrance of the Truth. I had soaked in these God-inspired words, promises, declarations, and commands many times before that night, but now, they lifted my heart and spirit as though I were hearing them for the first time. They felt brand-new yet strikingly familiar.

The peace washed over me but just as surely did the sickening foreboding of what would happen next as people heard the shocking news of Dad's suicide—on Christmas night, of all nights. How would they respond? Yet how might God use this tragedy in all sorts of different ways? How might he invite me to become intimately involved in that? How might I witness about the redeeming reality of God's plan, turning sin's tragedy to God's triumph?

Many times before that night, I had seen God fulfill his magnificent promises to use pain redemptively. I had experienced in my own life his "redemptive protocol," had watched him use my weeping to open a window into my heart and then through it, set me on the way closer to him. I had seen him use that protocol in the lives of others too as he opened the way to deeper truth and peace; as he offered to develop more loving, more real, deeper, and closer relationships, both with himself and with other people.

As I knelt there in the garden, I knew God was using even this experience as yet another answer to my many prayers that when suffering or crisis of any kind happened to people, God had placed in my sphere of influence that I would boldly and lovingly step into the gap for them, providing the hugs, help, and comfort that come from God's love and his True Truth. Firmly resting on the rock-solid foundation, being comforted by the Holy Spirit, and seeing the truths and falsehoods of my heart in a new way was the perfect setup for the way to move forward from here.

## Reentering the Chaos of Life: Take Careful Stock

***For the word of God is living and active, sharper than any two-edged sword, piercing to the division of soul and of spirit, of joints and of marrow, and discerning the thoughts and intentions of the heart.***
***(Heb. 4:12)***

My first book provided much more content to explore, exegete, and exercise these providentially provided and perfect set of passages from God's Scripture, but please carefully consider the summary principles and practices below. You'll note the basis for each Bible passage given to me by the Spirit has been expanded to include its context here.

As a preface for this segment of the Way, please consider another spin on the principle, the order, and the activity of how important moving back into the chaos is following

## TAKE HEART

any heartbreak and heart transformation of any kind: stay put, and beginning internally and with the counsel of Christ-centered people:

1) Mark.
2) Moan.
3) Marvel.
4) And then, and only then, Move out into the chaos; redeemed to redeem!

Beloved of God in Christ, following heartbreak of any kind or degree, even though every fiber of our being is tempting us to get back to normal, *the very last thing any Christ-centered Christian is…is normal!* Doctrinally, biblically screwed down tight, spiritually revived, and passionate, constructive revolutionaries are not normal folk. Avoiding the change of heart in store for us in God's plan of redemptive suffering will make us "normal"—just what Satan loves and God abhors:

*I know your works: you are neither cold nor hot. Would that you were either cold or hot! So, because you are lukewarm, and neither hot nor cold, I will spit you out of my mouth. For you say, I am rich, I have prospered, and I need nothing, [I'm living a comfortable life.] not realizing that you are wretched, pitiable, poor, blind, and naked. (Rev. 3:15–17, parenthesis added)*

1) Mark the change of heart: less stone, more flesh (Ezek. 11:17–21; 36).

2) Moan the purpose of the Spirit: less me, more Christ (Rom. 8:18–30).
3) Marvel the mercy of God: less whining, more worship (Rom. 11; 12:1–3).
4) Move the mountain with faith: less ruminating, more redeeming (Job 9; 19:25).

This is so doctrinal and life-givingly important: a Christian disciple is tested (1 Cor. 3:13), refined (Isa. 48:10), conformed (Rom. 8:29), made more like Christ by redemptive suffering (1 Pet. 4:12–19), and then must move back into the world of chaos, confusion, and calamity (Eph. 2:8–10). This truism at the core of God's plan of redemption is exponentially consequential. Why? Because redemptive suffering issues in spiritual fruit (Gal. 5:22–23) and an urgency to serve others (Matt. 20:28; Mark 10:45) more than almost anything else God includes in his perfect plan.

The Way is the Weeping and the Window exponentially added up and amassed for the purpose and benefit of "releasing the power of Christ in the re-born and renewed person" into the world of darkness and decay (please read that sentence again). Put another way, Martin Luther said, "Christians are 'little Christs.'" Following God's plan of redemptive suffering "makes little Christs into bigger Christs" so that the person and power of Christ grows and resounds in the world through us.

Please tell me, do you believe it would ever be possible to exhaust the manifold mercies of God contained in this principle and practice? Do you believe we could ever be thankful enough to God? Can you see why this part of the Gospel—the breadth and depth of God's mercies in Christ—is what angels long to gaze into (1 Pet. 1:12)?

So don't miss this one: Please, oh please, don't waste your tears. God knows how precious each one is to him, to you, and to this weeping world: "You [God] keep track of all my sorrows. You have collected all my tears in your bottle. You have recorded each one in your book" (Ps. 56:8). That's unspeakably amazing but actionable, right (Rom. 5:3–5; 8:28)? Suffering well stewarded is transformed into Christ's comfort spread abroad (2 Cor. 1:3–7).

Anticipation of moving back into chaos of a broken world can paralyze or crush us. But mourning is an absolutely vital aspect of what a wounded healer does. For a whole host of reasons, the vast majority of us can't wait to "get back to normal" after a heartbreak or free fall. But the Bible says, "Blessed are those who mourn, for they will be comforted" (Matt. 5:4) and that God comforts us "so that we will comfort others" (2 Cor. 1:3–7). More than anything, mourning is meant by God for "marking, moaning, marveling, and then moving." How does it work? Let's look at the Bible passages given me by the Spirit Christmas night.

## Mark the Change of Heart: Less Stone, More Flesh

*I will give them one heart, and a new spirit I will put within them. I will remove the heart of stone*

***from their flesh and give them a heart of flesh.***
***(Ezek.11:19)***

God offered the first verses from Ezekiel to remind me of the promise and fact of my conversion and continued sanctification. This was a doubly powerful reminder and verse to give me because of two amazing things: (a) it describes how my heart of sin-hardened stone was supernaturally removed when I first saw my blackened heart and sin and cried out to God to save me, twenty years before the night in Dad's garden, which prepared me to stand up, turn from my dad, and brokenly yet boldly move into the chaos of the world—as part of the family of God with no more shame; (b) but within this specific verse about how my heart had been supernaturally changed, there are two before and after verses that drifted through my heart about the first.

The context of Ezekiel 11:19 recapitulates the weeping/window/way protocol: setting us on the foundation of mercy; leading us to remove the idols that reside in our hearts; calling us to recommit our lives to God; and warning those who ignore such a marvelous and manifold mercy:

Weeping: Foundations of Mercy

***Thus says the Lord God: "I will gather you from the peoples and assemble you out of the countries where you have been scattered, and I will give you the land of Israel."***
***(Ezek. 11:17)***

# TAKE HEART

Window: Idol Work of the Heart

***And when they come there, they will remove from it all its detestable things and all its abominations. And I will give them one heart, and a new spirit I will put within them. I will remove the heart of stone from their flesh and give them a heart of flesh.***
***(Ezek. 11:18–19)***

Way: Recommitment to God

***That they may walk in my statutes and keep my rules and obey them. And they shall be my people, and I will be their God.***
***(Ezek. 11:20, emphasis added)***

Warning: To Those Who Ignore Such a Great Mercy

***But as for those whose heart goes after their detestable things and their abominations, I will bring their deeds upon their own heads," declares the Lord GOD.***
***(Ezek. 11:21, emphasis added)***

Check this out. Not only did God graciously prepare me to move out of the garden and into the world by reminding me of the reality of my conversion, but also he did so by using a verse whose context precisely expresses what I had experienced at the window: seeing truths, falsehoods (re: detestable things and abominations) of my true and false guilt in relationship to my dad and Jesus Christ (v. 18) and seeing my walk with God ("They shall be my people, and I will be their God") as one of love rather than condemnation (v. 20).

This new walk is a life continuously being transformed more and more into the likeness of Jesus. It's "more Jesus, less Adam" in me as I take advantage of *every* trial to discover where my temporal and everlasting joy can really be found (James 1).

Jesus said the following to his Father just before his ascension and imparting the Holy Spirit:

> **They [Jesus's disciples/Christians] are not of the world, just as I am not of the world. Sanctify them in the truth; your word is truth. As you sent me into the world, so I have sent them into the world. And for their sake I consecrate [set apart, dedicate] myself, that they also may be sanctified in truth.**
> **(John 17:16–19)**

God offered me a rich yet radically plain reminder that this time with him and Dad in the garden resulted in a "continuation of the transformation of my heart" that is as real as anything I, we, could ever imagine or hope for. I was not saved again but rather "saved from more and more worldliness" and sanctified for service. I can tell you straight from the heart, and with God as my witness, the metaphor of a stony heart being transformed into a soft, wholly alive heart is supernaturally initiated, entrusted to our obedient stewardship, and absolutely real—and the implications are spiritually, emotionally, psychologically, and physically radical, reliable, and relatable.

## TAKE HEART

So before I had to turn and leave Dad, God was saying in this verse, "John, do not ever discount what a change of heart only I can impart—for my glory, in you, and in the world! Forgetting this reality would be as detrimental as denying the change to the universe when I spoke it into existence or raised my Son from the dead. Please have faith in me to create the change of heart I promised, a heart set apart to change the world with me moving forward. A real change of heart is a vitally important thing, John. In fact, it's at the very center of my redemptive plan. A supernaturally and cathartically [emotionally purged] changed heart is what my Spirit's creative power in this broken world does to use trials to transform my people and, in due time, the universe as well. Do not suppress the change, for if you do, all of this will be wasted and your heart will be left needlessly hardened, deeply wanting, and further from me, beloved."

After seeing and feeling the transformation of heart that occurred in this timeless time with God and my dad, the clear challenge that lay ahead was daunting and real.

- When did or have you experienced the process of the transformation of your heart "from stone to flesh?" How did that change come about? What stony parts of your heart and life are still in need of transformation? What "fleshy parts" have been transformed that you could thank God for and tell others about?
- Think of someone who has known your heart in an authentic way for some time. How would this person say your heart has changed over the years?

- When have you marked the changes God was making and talked about this change of heart with someone else? What happened as a result? Why might a private versus public affirmation of a change of heart be important?
- Knowing how important community is to a change of heart, are you part of a committed, life-changing, and accountable community today? If no, what might be a few first steps in solidifying these sorts of relationship issues? If yes, is there an encouraging story of change that occurred in such a setting of community care, friendships for you?
- Consider how you would finish a sentence, paragraph, or commitment of this kind: "Moving back into the chaos of this world in the way God desires, I must closely consider and commit to…"

## Moan the Purpose of the Spirit: Less Me, More Christ

***We know that for those who love God, all things work together for good, for those who are called according to his purpose.***
***(Rom. 8:28)***

The good promised here refers first and foremost to the fact our Father intends we be conformed to the likeness of his Son (Rom. 8:29) as he works in and through everything he allows to happen in our lives. In giving me this verse, God was saying, "Trust me, John. The heartbreak we experienced together tonight did not take me by surprise. I saw it before time began, and I intend to use it for your

## TAKE HEART

good: to conform your heart, spirit, and life more to the likeness of my Son. And that's just the start to how I can and will use this tragedy. For many others will be affected as well."

Even as this truth washed over me, the Holy Spirit was interceding for me in my weakness (Rom. 8:26–27). God the Father answered the Spirit's intercession, responding to it perfectly. Through it all, the Spirit continued to point to Jesus. Within every trial endured and every tear shed by God's suffering servants, there exists manifold opportunities to participate in his redemptive work: less me, more Christ. Less you, more Christ. Less dark, more light. Less decay, more preservation. Less stone, more flesh. Less bitter, more better.

As I think about my dad and the tragedy of his death, I am tempted to say to God—as I'm sure you may have as well—"Even this? Even though the heartbreak will disfigure so many?"

But whenever I have mouthed that prayer, God has always spoken back to my heart, "No, John, *especially* this. I remake broken hearts, but I will not transform hearts hardened by self-sufficiency, hearts unavailable to me. You will not only see but will come to joyfully anticipate it as you know, grow, and sow. 'Consider this all joy'" (James 1:2). Honestly, I don't ask that question ["Even this?"] anymore. I know in the deepest recesses of my heart, "Especially this!"

"For those who are called according to his purpose." That's me. That's you. If you have repented of your sin and placed your faith in Jesus Christ as your Savior and Lord (of all aspects of your life, not just the aspects you decide to give him Lordship over), "all things work together for good." In Christ, we can trust God's promise. And when we do—if we're attentive, wise, and discerning—many times we will be treated to a proof of the promise by seeing transformed lives.

This oftentimes over or misused verse—Romans 8:28—was such a balm of remembrance for my shattered yet renewed heart. A sudden tragedy of this kind can appear to have no redeeming value whatsoever. But appearances from this world's perspective are vain at best and deceptively damning at worst.

God so generously reminded me I was one who—albeit highly imperfectly, loved God and was called according to his purpose—would experience again and again how God would use this tragedy for his triumph and the blessing of many, many people.

This reminder of God's rock-solid and trustworthy promise to use all things for the good of those who love him was huge for me, especially as I faced turning and leaving my dad lying cold and dying in the snow and walking into chaos and a flood of tears. I was safely in the arms of God, who would open hearts to himself again and again and again. Do you have a heartfelt trust, and perhaps some concrete examples, that God will work all things together for your good, leading to the good of others?

With these ideas from Romans 8 in mind, please reflect on these questions:

## *TAKE HEART*

- After a tragedy, it's so easy to stand at a spiritual distance and say something like, "We know that in all things, God works for the good of those who love him." Or more commonly in our culture, "everything happens for a reason." In what specific ways, though, have you seen God work through a tragedy for genuine good in your life and through you in the life of someone you know? Be as specific as possible.
- Have you heard someone quote this familiar passage in times of suffering? What has been your response? What is your reaction when you hear that God intends to use all the things he allows in your life for your good?
- Does conforming you to the likeness of Jesus Christ and redeeming the ruin in many possible ways appeal to you, inspire you, mystify you, scare you, and/or alienate you in any way? If yes, why? If no, why not?
- Is God, even now, opening a window into your heart? If so, what do you see through it? Ask the Holy Spirit to show you. Invite a trusted friend to listen as well.
- Immediately after a trial, words fail. A hug or what some have called "the ministry of presence" is the first step in heart triage. In the longer term, though, in what ways could you come alongside someone whose heart has been crushed when God has opened a window into the heart and is ready to show his child the way?

- Consider how you would finish a sentence, paragraph, or commitment of this kind: "Moving back into the chaos of this world in the way God desires, I will closely consider and commit to…"

## Marvel the Mercy of God: Less Whining, More Worship

*Do not be conformed to this world, but be transformed by the renewal of your mind, that by testing you may discern what is the will of God, what is good and acceptable and perfect.*
*(Rom. 12:2)*

In these words, I heard a sweet remembrance and an admonition of love for my heart, spirit, and will directly from the Spirit. God was saying, in essence, "Use this time and the trauma of heartbreak as an occasion for remembering, John. Remember your citizenship in the world to which you really belong. Remember you are mine, and you will be richly blessed if you move back into the material world being in it but not of it" (Matt. 16:26; John 1:10; 17; Col. 2:8).

In Romans 11, Paul describes the hardness of heart shown by those whose hearts *should* have been the most responsive to God's mercies. Old Testament Israel had seen that mercy at work on their behalf time after time. Yet rather than falling to their knees in worship, they fell into temptation of grumbling and complaining—re: *whining*—about God's provision for them.

## TAKE HEART

God hates whining. Their hearts became harder and harder, and their tears watered the seeds of idolatry Satan had sown. Still, to Paul's stunned amazement, God's mercy was active even in judgment. Despite their sins, "all Israel," those who live and die in the faith, will be saved (Rom. 11:26; see also Gal. 6:16).

God's clear message is this: responding to trials and the manifold mercies of God by heart-hardening whining is never a good idea. In fact, it's a heart killer.

Not only repentant Jews, but also faith-filled Gentiles will taste the mercy of God despite their sinful depravity. Chapter 11 concludes with an expression of deep worship and Paul's near-dumbfounded astonishment at this mercy in worshipful amazement and not hard-hearted whining:

*Oh, the depth of the riches and wisdom and knowledge of God! How unsearchable are his judgments and how inscrutable his ways! For who has known the mind of the Lord, or who has been his counselor? ... For from him and through him and to him are all things.*
*To him be glory forever. Amen.*
*(Rom.11:33–36)*

You might want to repeat this verse: like the author Paul, does the spirit of outright full-bore—"Oh!"—worship touch your heart? The more we are transformed by the redemptive use of our trials, the more we break out in unashamed, unabashed worship of this kind. We just can't help it: "Oh, Father, Son, and Holy Spirit, help me see the breadth and depth of your glory."

Please take heart and know this: we comprehend the experience and measure of God's love and mercy in direct proportion to the degree we know our own sinfulness and the wrath we justly deserve because of it. Knowing then our culpability and its rightful penalty, we join Paul in his hymn of praise as chapter 11 ends and chapter 12 begins:

> ***I appeal to you therefore, brothers, by the mercies of God, to present your bodies as a living sacrifice, holy and acceptable to God, which is your spiritual worship. Do not be conformed to this world, but be transformed by the renewal of your mind, that by testing you may discern what is the will of God, what is good and acceptable and perfect.***
> ***(Rom.12:1)***

Have you ever made the mistake of forgetting the menace of your own heart while downplaying the depth and breadth of God's mercy, saying or thinking something like, "God is not listening to my prayers or taking my agenda into account. I only want what I deserve. I can't believe this is happening to me while Heaven remains silent and my prayers bounce off the ceiling of my bedroom. Why can't I get through to him? Why aren't my needs being met for once?"

I have heard words like these from my own lips and have seen this attitude in my own heart more times than I'd like to admit. The Bible equates my whining with a grumbling spirit and explicitly forbids it (Exod. 16; John 6:43, 61; 1 Pet. 4:9). Yours too. The alternative to this "road to nowhere," sanctified suffering transforms (recreates by the

Spirit) our perspective on life and death. It cleanses our hearts of the hardness that leads us to grumble, whine, and complain and replaces *grumbling* with *gratitude*. By God's design, redemptive suffering is his main action plan to transform grumbling into gratitude.

*For by the grace given to me I say to everyone among you, not to think of himself more highly than he ought to think, but to think with sober judgment, each according to the measure of faith that God has assigned ... Let love be genuine. Abhor what is evil; hold fast to what is good. Love one another with brotherly affection. Outdo one another in showing honor. Do not be slothful in zeal, be fervent in spirit, serve the Lord. Rejoice in hope, be patient in tribulation, be constant in prayer. Contribute to the needs of the saints and seek to show hospitality.*

*Bless those who persecute you; bless and do not curse them. Rejoice with those who rejoice, weep with those who weep. Live in harmony with one another. Do not be haughty, but associate with the lowly. Never be wise in your own sight. Repay no one evil for evil, but give thought to do what is honorable in the sight of all. If possible, so far as it depends on you, live peaceably with all.*

*Beloved, never avenge yourselves, but leave it to the wrath of God, for it is written, "Vengeance is mine, I will repay, says the Lord." To the contrary, "if your enemy is hungry, feed him; if he is*

*thirsty, give him something to drink; for by so doing you will heap burning coals on his head."*
*(Rom.12:3, 9–20)*

Then, in one simple, culminating sentence, Paul sums it all up:

**Do not be overcome by evil,
but overcome evil with good.
(Rom.12:21)**

We are all made to be transformed as we marvel the mercy of God with less whining, more worship. Grace, worship, and Christian growth go hand in hand as do their opposites: grabbing, grumbling, and immaturity. In short, the inevitable suffering we experience leads us to either be overcome by evil (bitter) or overcome evil with good (better).

After a heart-shattering trial, getting back to normal is not even an option. Instead, suffering offered to God as we die to ourselves will result in lives of worship, cruciform (cross-shaped) lives that lift worship to God and simultaneously reach out to sufferers near us (Luke 10:27). It's really all about a new normal.

Jesus's words teach exactly this:

*Abide in my love. If you keep my commandments, you will abide in my love, just as I have kept my Father's commandments and abide in his love. These things I have spoken to you, that my joy may be in you, and that your joy*

# TAKE HEART

*may be full.*
*(John 15:4)*

**Beloved, let us love one another, for love is from God, and whoever loves has been born of God and knows God. Anyone who does not love does not know God, because God is love. In this the love of God was made manifest among us, that God sent his only Son into the world, so that we might live through him.**
*(1 John 4:7–9)*

As you can see, worship means much more than simply going to church on Sunday, though that certainly plays a central part in our redeemed lives. The Bible properly defines worship as both a lifestyle and an attitude of the heart that, together, result in God's glory, the believer's good, and other's being blessed.

**Do not be conformed to this world, but be transformed by the renewal of your mind, that by testing you may discern what is the will of God, what is good and acceptable and perfect.**
*(Rom.12:2)*

With this in mind, let these questions guide your reflection:

- In your own words, try to reframe what "Marvel the mercy of God: less whining, more worship" means to you.
- "Conformed [to this world] or transformed [by renewing of your mind]." What evidence can you cite to show that God allows trials, in part, to remind us we are not citizens of this world but

rather "resident-aliens" (John 17:16; Phil. 3:20)? How might this remembering play out in your community of family, faith, friendships, etc.?

- In Christ, you bring to the world the best, most enduring solutions to the woes of the world. How does knowing that fill you with a humble confidence? A contented urgency? A passionate compassion?
- How confident are you that you know God's good, acceptable, and perfect will for your life? Explain. How might you cultivate growth in that confidence? How might others help you along the journey?
- How passionate are you for God's redemptive plan? In light of the fact that those who follow the patterns of this world are doomed to live lives of failure, frustration, and futility, how do you respond when you see those who don't know Christ making this heart-damaging choice?
- When do you most often resort to grumbling and complaining? What might be "the sin beneath the sin" (where God is replaced by certain specific idols, lesser gods) stoking the fire of discontent? List five ways you might investigate and address this.
- If you were to set a course with a community of Christians you trust, committed to helping one another avoid being "conformed to the patterns of this world" but instead "transformed by the renewing of your mind[s]," what would it look like?

How might you go about it? Be as detailed as possible.
- Consider how you would finish this sentence: "Moving back into the chaos of this world in the way God desires, I will closely consider and commit to…"

## Move the Mountain with Faith: Less Ruminating, More Redeeming

The 180-degree turn from our suffering to face a world of chaos, confusion, and calamity is incredibly important for us not just to do, but to dwell on—and dwell on with a "holy intention" by faith, and in community. This turning, this about-face, is indeed the same principle and practice of being born again by repenting, coming to faith, leaving behind a sin-driven life, and turning from idols to serving King Jesus.

*Repent therefore, and turn back, that your sins may be blotted out, that times of refreshing may come from the presence of the Lord, and that he may send the Christ appointed for you, Jesus, whom Heaven must receive until the time for restoring all the things about which God spoke by the mouth of his holy prophets long ago. (Acts 3:19–21)*

As I made my own turn that Christmas night to face a world of chaos, God gave me one last passage, which promised a deep hope and prepared me to take the first step into the chaos, tender in heart yet radically tenacious about wanting to see how God would use everything that had happened for the good he had promised:

**[Job said,] I know my Redeemer lives, and at the last he will stand upon the earth. (Job 19:25)**

Outside of Jesus himself, Job endured more suffering than anyone else in Scripture. As I thought about the words Job wrote so long ago, two key truths echoed through my mind:

1) I know...Jesus Christ, my Redeemer King, lives. *He really and truly lives.* Death, sin, Satan, and hell could not hold him captive. That's the True Truth.
2) I know...the gift of salvation and the eventual resurrection with Christ upon his second coming, which I have received by faith, is *not* an end in itself. Rather, it provides the impulse and power that enables me to work with Jesus as a co-redeemer in an increasingly broken world until I die or he returns.

Before any of us step back into the chaos as more transformed and committed co-redeemers in Christ, we should be absolutely sure of exactly how we would finish the declaration and battle cry, "I know."

Matthew Henry comments true and well on Job 19:25 and the context in which it's written:

*The Spirit of God, at this time, seems to have powerfully wrought on the mind of Job. Here he witnessed a good confession; declared the soundness of his faith, and the assurance of his hope. Here is much*

# *TAKE HEART*

*of Christ and Heaven; and he that said such things are these, declared plainly that he sought the better country, that is, the heavenly. Job was taught of God to believe in a living Redeemer; to look for the resurrection of the dead, and the life of the world to come; he comforted himself with the expectation of these.*

Job prophesied the Messiah's victory over suffering and death. He was assured he had a living Redeemer who would come in the flesh, accomplish salvation, and on the last day appear as the Judge of the world, raise the dead, and complete the redemption of his people. May these faithful sayings be engraved by the Holy Spirit upon our hearts.

Significantly, Job penned these words not after, but during his trial. He wrote while he wept. He wrote not in spite of, but because of his suffering. Note how Henry acknowledges that Job's faith had a rock-solid foundation before he was sorely tested by God. Job's faith was mightily rooted by the person and power of the Holy Spirit and an eternal view of life so that the winds of unavoidable suffering could not blow him away.

Job was made momentarily bitter by the wrongheaded theology of his "friends" but by chapter 38 was reminded of the basis of his faith and, in the end, made better by God. By means of Job's weeping (Job 16:16), window (Job 19:3–5; 40:4–5), and way (Job 42), he emerges from the free fall's refining fire as even purer gold, as more humble yet bold, as more devoted to God, as a greater witness of God's wonder than he could have ever dared imagine. He proclaimed the Word, and so can we:

*Oh that my words were written! Oh that they were inscribed in a book! Oh that with an iron pen and lead they were engraved in the rock forever! For I know that my Redeemer lives, and at the last he will stand upon the earth. And after my skin has been thus destroyed, yet in my flesh I shall see God, whom I shall see for myself, and my eyes shall behold, and not another! My heart faints within me!*
*(Job 19:23–27)*

Yes, Job wavered but, in the end, remained faithful not just even, but especially, as he endured unimaginable suffering. He took comfort in God's character and in the hope of his own resurrection, and it transformed his heart to ramp-up the breadth and depth of his faith (re: Job 38–41, leading up to Job 42, where Job expresses his renewed commitment to God and his faith) and invested in transforming others.

## We Have Been Redeemed to Redeem

As I stood, turned, and walked into the chaos, the Spirit quietly, lovingly yet undeniably repeated, "Redeemed to redeem. Redeemed to redeem. Redeemed to redeem."

No aspect of that Christmas night with my dad and God was intended for me alone. Instead, the words *redeemed to redeem* circled and cut though my heart and spirit, propelling me forward into the chaos with a radically renewed purpose of heart. No sanctified suffering of any kind belongs only to the sufferer. God redeemed my weeping for the explicit purpose of redeeming and comforting others who weep. Because, by the person and power of the Holy Spirit, he lives in us; we can love and accompany any others who sit at the open *window* of their hearts, seeking the *way* the Holy Spirit would use to help them live more fully the life of Jesus.

That purpose makes it possible to awaken every morning and fall asleep every night, knowing my life's purpose as a co-redeemer with Christ. When we see our suffering through this lens, we can pray as Jesus taught—"Our Father, who art in heaven, hallowed be thy name. Thy Kingdom come, Thy will be done on earth as it is in heaven"—and then let him make us part of the answer to our own prayer. We see the kingdom come as the Redeemer works in and with us and empowers us to cut through the chaos and offer to others the compassion of Christ we ourselves have experienced. What a far cry from being confused, hardened, and bitter about why God allows suffering to occur! Christians are saved and sanctified *in order to be sent*.

By means of your trials, how has the Redeemer begun his radical transformation in your heart? Have you begun to act as a co-redeemer with Christ, as one who lives out the True Truth that the Triune God lives in you, that your Redeemer lives forever, and that weeping has opened a window in your heart and you have seen the way God intends to use your tears for his divine purposes?

You have been redeemed—by God, in Christ, through the power of the Holy Spirit—to move mountains, beloved. Every person who has ever walked into your life has been sent by God to receive a compassionate and redemptive word or deed from Jesus Christ through you. Every person. Think of it. When our hardness of heart, self-focus, or fear causes us to pass up these opportunities, we can develop deep remorse. I know. I've been there often. But I do it a lot less often today because by God's grace at work in my heart, I'm more wholly conformed, unafraid, compassionate, and committed to step into the chaos.

Praise God he used the weeping, the window, and the way to revolutionize my life. He can revolutionize yours too. I pray he does by way of your unavoidable suffering and all the sanctification the Spirit has in store for you. I pray with all my heart that all of God's people will engage less in useless ruminating and grow more redemptively responsive to his call: "Today, if you hear God's voice, do not harden your heart" (Ps. 95:7–8; Heb. 3:7, 15).

If there is a call upon God's people today, it could be put like this: "Stop the ruminating, questioning, wondering, and whining about God, and get to the business and ministry of *redeeming* in every sphere of your life."

The apostle Paul put it in even more plain and admonishing words:

***When I was a child, I spoke like a child, I thought like a child, I reasoned like a child. When I became a man, I gave up childish ways.
(1 Cor. 13:11)***

***So that we may no longer be children, tossed to and fro by the waves and carried about by every***

*wind of doctrine, by human cunning, by craftiness in deceitful schemes. Rather, speaking the truth in love, we are to grow up in every way into him who is the head, into Christ.*
*(Eph. 4:14–15)*

## Job: On the Other Side of Suffering

Now transformed, renewed, readied, and redeemed, I humbly, brokenly yet boldly, and expectantly moved out from this sacred time into an increasingly dark, misshapen, and chaotic world. In the last verse, God graciously reminded me, "I am your Redeemer King, and you are a co-redeemer, John. My Spirit Counselor, my disciples, and the church will be with you as you have been powerfully present in a wretched yet redeeming time so that you will be able to help redeem this sad, sickened, and suffering world. You have been redeemed much in this time of heart-shattering woe so that I may be glorified and you might be a more committed servant of me. Yes, 'redeemed to redeem'—that is what this message means."

God graciously reminded me as he walked me back through it all again: "In Creation, I created, and now sustain, this world. I sent my Son to be sacrificed for the freedom from the bondage of sin. I chose never to leave or forsake you—ever. I offer saved sinners a window to see their heart as I do—as more sinful and yet more loved—so that one can choose more clearly to move back in to the chaos as a Christ-like redeeming force for my love and truth. In suffering, I mercifully offer a change of heart, faith and life, which empowers the assurance and hope to see me work by promise and paradox—that my ways are not man's ways.

"Finally, as you move closer and closer to a place in me as your beloved Redeemer King and Crown, you will be increasingly used as a co-redeemer. This is at the heart of my plan of redemption. I give you this mantle of co-redeemer in Christ. Move out now—humbly yet boldly, in truth and love, intentionally compassionate, sword drawn and readied—into the chaos. My light of truth and salt of preserving and healing in you is more needed than ever."

I stood up, shaking and weak, to greet the crush of the world. In the next few moments, I answered many questions for the police and EMTs, haggled with the paramedics about where to take Dad, told my stepmother, Marge, I would see her at the ER, and then stepped into a police car. It was blessedly warm. I sat silent, sapped, and stunned for quite some time. The young officer and I watched several large fire trucks jockey for position among the nearly dozen vehicles struggling to leave the tight, snow-filled lane.

I don't know how long the silence and the waiting lasted before I broke it. Without turning my head, still staring into the flashing lights in the lane, I asked the officer, "Do you have a faith in Jesus Christ?"

Almost without hesitation, he answered, "Yes. Yes, I do."

I responded just as quickly, "Awesome." Then I followed up with a second question, "Are you sure your folks do too?"

## TAKE HEART

He thought for a moment. "I'm pretty sure they do," he said finally. "But I should make sure. Sometimes, a person can just assume these things. We sometimes don't talk about the most important things in life with those we love until it's too late. I'll make sure ..." His voice trailed off.

At those words, my weeping welled up, I released a quiet whimper, and I shuddered in amazement and tearful joy. I couldn't help myself. Somehow the officer knew my heart's deep hurt. Somehow God was at work. Perhaps the tragedy had opened a window in the young officer's heart, a window into some unchallenged assumptions and dark corners, corners that had remained unexplored or even closed to the weeping of others. That thought triggered an incredible rush.

A deep chill ran up and down my spine. A rush of hope flooded my heart as tears overflowed my eyes and ran down my face. I was overwhelmed at the sudden realization that the redemptive promise God had given me *not moments before in the garden* was already being fulfilled!

New shoots of God's redeeming love had already begun to poke through the white, cold snow and the dark ashes of this awful night of the soul. Already God was redeeming these terrible events. Through the tears, I closed my eyes, lowered my head, and smiled at the down payment God had just made—already made—on his promise. Silently, I thanked God that even if nothing else positive came out of it, one heart, perhaps even more, had potentially changed for time and for eternity. My Redeemer really and truly does live right now, even in the midst of this horrid mess.

Please let the questions below guide you as you reflect and journal:

1) Being redeemed to redeem must begin by being born again. There is no possibility of experiencing this power devoid of repenting of our sin from the heart and beseeching Christ to be our Savior from hell and the Lord of our life. Have you been born again and begun the journey of the Christian faith as a co-redeemer in Christ?

2) All of us have a tendency to ruminate or resist God, resulting in half-hearted, lukewarm, or fearful lives. Can you name the areas of your faith life that are in bondage to ruminating and not at liberty for co-redeeming?

3) If you were to write the most important things in your life in a list from 1 to 5, all beginning with "I know," what would you write and be willing to share with someone who would help you live them out each day?

4) In what ways do you see yourself as a person being redeemed to redeem? Comforted to comfort? Saved to save/serve? Plucked out of hell to help rescue others? Fed to feed? Loved to give love? Having had tears wiped away to wipe away other's tears? A wounded healer?

5) How might better knowing the *Redeemer* energize you for your daily calling as a *co-redeemer*? What's at the heart of any rumination, resistance, or reluctance you may feel when considering this possibility?

6) Job, in faith-filled suffering, wrote, "Oh that my words were written! Oh that they were inscribed in a book! Oh that with an iron pen and lead they were engraved in the rock forever!" If you were to feel a passion like that about your life in Christ, what would you write? How would you attempt to be intentional about such ideas and words coming to fruition?

7) When have you seen the way closer to Jesus in a time of deep weeping? What was that like for you? How might God want to use you to comfort others by means of your own experiences with weeping and windows?

8) In what ways would you like to be more like Jesus as your heart is conformed to his likeness (consider Philippians 2:1–11; Galatians 5:16–26; Colossians 3:1–25; and 1 John 2:6)? How might a regular time for fasting, adoration, confession, thanksgiving, and supplication help you? Please be explicit.

## God's People Are Called to Move into the Chaos Every Day

*We are not wise enough, pure enough, or strong enough to aim and sustain such a single motive over a lifetime. That way lies fanaticism or failure. But if the single motive is the master motivation of God's calling, the answer is yes. In any and all situations, both today and tomorrow's tomorrow, God's call to us is the unchanging and ultimate whence, what, why, and whither of our lives. Calling is a 'yes' to God that carries a 'no' to the chaos of modern demands. Calling is the key to tracing the story line of our lives and unriddling*

*JOHN O. DOZIER, JR.*

*the meaning of our existence in a chaotic world.
(Os Guinness, The Call: Finding and Fulfilling the Central Purpose of Your Life)*

# In Closing
# Take Close and Careful Stock of Your Heart

## God's Protocol for Redemptive Suffering: Just for You

I was recently reminded of all the Bible authors (mostly everyone) who resorted to a common heartfelt and compassionate plea to God's people: "Let me remind you." (A few New and Old Testament examples are the following: 1 Chronicles 16:15; Psalm 111:5; Jeremiah 31:33–34; 1 Corinthians 15:1–3; 2 Timothy 1:6; 2:8; and 2 Peter 1:12–21, which is in part below).

Repentant, reborn Christians—made wise and urgently compassionate by redemptive suffering—exhibit the following: (a) they are reminded by God, (b) they remind themselves, and (c) they remind one another often. By "speaking the truth in love" (Eph. 4:15), it's what Christ's disciples do—to the church, believers, and then to those who might listen in the world.

As the passage from 2 Peter below reminds us, even though the church knows and/or is supposed to know the Gospel truth about their faith, we need to remember and remind one another of it each and every day:

*Therefore I intend always to remind you of these qualities, though you know them and are established in the truth that you have. I think it right, as long as I am in this body, to stir you up by way of reminder, since I know that the putting off of my body will be soon, as our Lord Jesus Christ made clear to me. And I will make every effort so that after my departure you may be able at any time to recall these things.*
*(2 Peter 1:12–15)*

Yes, even "though you know them and are established in the truth that you have," again and again, the Bible calls us to remember. And for very good reason: we have either never known or forgotten a great deal of what we once knew. (This is especially true in an era of more unchurched churchgoers than ever.) Therefore, even if review feels repetitious, it is required.

Both the Western culture at large, the lion's share of its institutions and policies, and even the church, I'm afraid, have been living in a culture of comfort for a long while. The roots of postmodernism, rampant secularization, and life without knowing and giving attention to God are firmly entrenched ways of our culture.

"Reversing the curse of our many blessings of comfort" is not just impossible devoid of returning to the Triune God and the True Truth of biblical doctrine, but even if and when we do, it takes quite a long time to dig around the deeply entrenched roots to bring a godly and fruitful life back to the church and society: We not only have to *remember* but also remember and remember and remember again and again—for generations—in order to "re-member", re-unite and re-send the Church.

God longs to see a new time for us and our churches when joy comes with trials (James 1:2–4; 1 Pet. 5:10); when weeping engenderers worship (Rom. 5:3–5); when suffering is treasured for the sanctifying changes it provides (1 Thess. 5:23; 2 Tim. 2:21); when sowing tears reaps more abundant joy (Ps. 126:5); when our daily mission includes comforting others with the comfort given us (2 Cor. 1:3–7); when more church leaders are more self-aware concerning their own story of redemptive suffering and are less ambivalent or afraid to be real with the flock about heartbreaking and redeeming issues (1 Pet. 5:1–5; 1 Tim. 3:1–16); and when crisis is processed for the conformity to Christ it's meant to achieve (Rom. 8:18; 1 Pet. 4:12–19).

## A Plea to Know and Remember the Condition of Your Heart before the Next Heartbreak Occurs

We've looked at this before, but it's worth saying in the most urgent, loving, and truthful way again: Have you been born again? Do you have a new heart made alive by the person and power of the Holy Spirit? Have you reached the point of being real about God's perfection, your imperfection, your need of repentance and a Savior and Lord of your life? Do you have a conversion story, a time in your life where you can say you began a radical journey of faith in God's Son, Jesus Christ, and shifted from a *proposition* to believe into a *penitent* person of God—and self-awareness? Have you had a life-changing change of heart about your life and God's role in it?

Every single human being lives under the pale of a very broken world as born into Adam's Sin and sinning habitually. It's not about if but when heartbreak will occur. But what makes all the difference in the universe is the condition of your heart when life's tiny or tumultuous trials make a dent, bruise, or break your heart. "Above all else, guard your heart, for it is the wellspring of [all] life [for time and eternity]" (Prov. 4:23—parenthesis added).

Please consider in another way your times of *weeping, the window* into your heart, and the *way* in which you are then better prepared to reenter the chaos, like Jesus Christ did and does still today:

## Your Weeping (Gen. 1:1; John 1:1; Deut. 31:6)

1) Do you believe that this statement "All weeping, all tears, all trials, and all free falls are God's offer for revealing and firming up the foundations of your faith?" is true?
2) Do you believe that all of humanity lives in a broken world where little and big free falls occur every day, 24-7, 365? That everyone we come into contact with is in some sort of free fall either personally or by someone else's pain of some kind?
3) Good news? All human beings have a God-made and God-shaped hole in his or her heart. Bad news? All human beings have a free will choice to

either fill the void with the Only God of the Bible or substitute it with lesser gods or idols. Do you believe every human being has placed their faith in something because that's the nature of what being human is about? And do you believe that trials test the nature and worthiness of everyone's faith foundations? All the worldly, devilish, and our sin-based foundations will absolutely fail us every time. Has God, you, and a community of faith placed you on the path and journey of firming up the foundations of your life and anyone whom God has placed in your proximity?

4) Do you believe that based upon the miraculous intervention on Christmas night, and far more importantly the Bible itself, God has established a "three-pillared foundation" for those who have come to faith in his Son Jesus Christ: (a) Creation: God created and sustains all things (Gen. 1:1 and following); (b) Christ: God sent his Son into the world as "the second Adam" to live a perfect life, die for the sins of the world on the cross [those who believe in him], say "It is finished," and be resurrected from the dead (John 1:1); and (c) Covenant: God made an unbreakable covenant promise by paying man's cost [in sin] and his own cost [in justice] to achieve a promise every human being wants most to feel each day: "Be strong and courageous; don't be terrified or afraid of them. For it is the Lord your God who goes with you; He will never, ever leave you or forsake you" (Deut. 31:6)?

5) Do you believe this three-pillar foundation God has established for his children is not only a *rock-solid force* against *the free falls of life* but also (a) "soil" into which the roots of our faith life grow more deeply every day and yield the fruit of the spirit as well as (b) act as a *platform* for why and how we exist on the earth until we die or Christ returns to make all things new?

6) Do you believe that "growing into and pressing into" and meditating on scripture in reference to Creation, Christ, Covenant, while being in a community of faith, will mature you and make you more and more like Jesus Christ?

7) Do you believe that Shalom peace, the temporal and eternal rest, the contentment and deepest satisfaction(s), and the reason for life each day that God the Father, Son, and Holy Spirit want for your life is impossible to obtain devoid of living your life upon the foundations God has made for your life? For all of human life?

8) Which provisions and promises from Scripture prove foundational for you when you experience emotions like fear, anxiety, worry, self-doubt, or trepidation of any kind? When has God kept his promises to you personally? (Name several specific events.)

9) Do you see that when [not if] trials come your way, there exists the most lofty and the most practical ways of going more deeply into Creation, Christ, and Covenant (e.g., "I just got some bad news about my health. I'm going to begin by going

outside, raising my gaze to the sky and at God's awesome creation, taking a deep breath, and reminding myself of God's creating and sustaining my self, my security, and all my solace.")?

10) Bless it forward: If you have received and you are internalizing "The Weeping: Free Falls and Foundations," please know it's meant to be given away (2 Cor. 1:3–7). How? By regularly applying the ministries of prayer, listening (first to understand), and speaking the truth in love [to let God be understood]. Without exception, every person God providentially places in your life is experiencing a free fall of some kind. Yes, the timing and order of magnitude and impact varies, but your ministry as a wounded healer (Nouwen) is to (a) pray for the Spirit's intervention; (b) reflectively listen, spiritually and emotionally discern, and genuinely and lovingly draw out the deeper-level goings-on; and (c) speak the truth in love, love truthfully by offering God's person and foundational truths about him and the person he has placed in your path. Wounded healers sense (see, hear, taste, touch, smell) free falls (hurts of any kind) and respond by lovingly and truthfully *reminding* others of God's foundations (the multifaceted realms of his Creation, Christ, and Covenant).

*JOHN O. DOZIER, JR.*

## Your Window (Rom. 1:18; Rom. 8:1)

1) Do you believe that once you are converted, born again and resting on the rock-solid foundation of Creation, Christ, and Covenant, you are assured no *punishment* is involved in your trial but only, only, only *purification*? That, in Christ, your sin (in Adam) and sinning (by habit) past, present, and future were taken care of on the cross by Jesus Christ's propitiating, atoning, substitutionary "It is finished" (John 19:30) death?

2) Do you believe that the inevitable trials of living life in a horribly broken world vary in the duration and depth of pain associated with each experience? But also that each should be seen and understood at a heart, depth, and breadth level before we try and "move on," "get back to life," or help anyone else do the same?

3) Do you believe that the purification (1 John 1:9; 1 Cor. 6:19–20), and softening (Ezek. 11:17–21; 36:26; John 17:21) of the heart is all about replacing falsehoods with True Truth—and gaining God, self, and other awareness for the purpose of being more Christ-like? And that it can be very difficult but vitally necessary?

4) Have you experienced various sorts of post-pain "would-a, could-a, should-a's," true and false guilt, and various regrets that have hardened your heart and made you bitter rather than better? If so, is the freedom offered by the gospel of Jesus Christ— going deeper into the depth of sin and the heights

of God's love—more attractive all the time? Have you been in that hellish place where regrets, true guilt, false guilt, and a maelstrom of emotional ambivalence dominate and own your life?

5) Do you see that purification is about "staying put at the blown-open window of your heart" for the purposes of opening the well-sealed compartments of your past; searching your heart; discerning between the falsehoods and truths of your life and faith; and explicitly routing out *falsehoods* to be replaced by the *Bible's truth*? How convicted are you that doing an inventory and a cleansing of the heart is what the Spirit supernaturally—and a community of faith incarnationally—helps to achieve as the Counselor, Pointer to Jesus, and the "Supernatural Heart-Changer?"

6) Do you believe mourning is, in large part, to "Stay put!", "pause at the window of the heart for a while?" Why do you believe this "pause" with the Spirit, a fellow Christian, or counselor is a natural and much-needed journey, process, and yet so difficult, even for the people of God? Might it have to do with "the habits of the heart" in living in a culture of shame, fear and comfort—which Jesus has eradicated if you have been born again?

7) Do you believe that even though the Holy Spirit and Scriptures are a vital part of this process and time at the shattered window looking deeply into the heart that God provided the Body of Christ in the church—"flesh-on-flesh" relationships speaking the truth in love—to come alongside,

listen, help, and counsel as well? That the only people who are truly objective will readily admit their subjectivity? That we are foolhardy, unnecessarily fearful, and wasteful of our heartbreak if we embark on the journey of redemptive suffering alone?

8) What are the roadblocks that keep you from trusting in God's promises more? When and where did those roadblocks originate?

9) Can you say with most of your heart (75 percent assurance) this sort of cathartic cleansing, purifying, help-toward-holiness, maturing, wisdom-making, transformative, world-changing, and Christ-conforming work in the heart is one of the most important parts of God's plan of redemption?

10) Bless it forward: If you have received and are internalizing The Window: More Sinful Yet More Loved, know it's meant to be given away (2 Cor. 1:3–7). How? By regularly applying the ministries of prayer, listening (first to understand), and speaking the truth in love (to let God be understood). It's a tender and ticklish time: A person God has sent into your life is weeping in a free fall of faith and fear; foundations need to be identified, replaced, shored up, or renewed; but not long after, we can be used of God to (a) pray about the window of the heart to stay open, for the Spirit to counsel, and be used to peer through into the realms of the heart (worldview, core beliefs, Christ centeredness, lesser gods, anxieties, fears, hopes,

etc., (b) reflectively listen to the wounded, weeping person about various truths and/or falsehoods flowing from his or her heart and emotions, and then (c) biblically, gently, patiently, intentionally, compassionately speak God's truth in love—his love in truth. Ultimately, your role and goal as a wounded healer, at the window of the heart of and with another wounded person, is the same as it is with your own heart: to listen and discern (1) what words, beliefs, values, self-worth, hopes, disappointments, joys, etc., *underpin, establish, reflect,* and *reinforce* the Gospel\* and (2) what words, beliefs, values, self-worth, hopes, disappointments, joys, etc., *undermine, disestablish, cloud,* and *refute* the Gospel\*. [\*The Gospel: "I am more sinful than ever imagine, and yet, I am more loved than I could ever dare hope for."]

11) Will you accept the amazing and most honorable calling as a Wounded Healer to help reinforce and encourage what is *true* about the Gospel in another's heart as well as what is *false*?

## Your Way (Ezek. 11:19; Rom. 8:28; 12:2; Job 19:25)

For the reasons expressed earlier, God the Spirit blessed me (and will bless you) with his scriptures before I left my father's side in the garden on Christmas night in order to turn and walk humbly, yet boldly, into the chaos of this broken world. As I expressed in my original book, the content and exposition of the passages I received are very rich, robust, and too much for us to dig into again here. So please, let me just remind you of the gist of each of the four passages—and God's call upon your life—if you desire to do his will and play a major role as a co-redeemer in Christ.

Sufferers who follow God's protocol for the weeping and the window, and do not waste their tears but let the Holy Spirit use them most redemptively, will likely then find the way forward to a vitally important phase of the journey.

Why? *It's the stage that can change the world.* But it's also the stage that our own still-sinful *flesh* resists, the *devil* abhors, and the *world* shuns. The way forward begins after the free-falling stops, the foundation is renewed, the heart renovation has begun, and we get back to our lives. As we do that, we do it as changed children of God with a radically renewed sense of mission in Christ: Saved. Sanctified. Urged to serve in Jesus's name.

It's vitally important to mark the change and differences that have occurred in our hearts and lives and begin to look for ways to use them for good in the lives of others. This will also help protect us from slipping back into the heart-hardening process Satan would so like to reestablish in our hearts. Reentry is not easy. Remember, you're a different person plunging back into the culture of comfort, a culture that does not want to notice changes in others for fear they might need to change themselves. This can and does even happen within the church, where many have become so accustomed to discomfort avoidance and a lukewarm sort of faith they are skeptical, if not resentful, of someone whose heart has been set on fire for the things of God.

## TAKE HEART

Following the miraculous experience of being with God and Dad in the garden on Christmas night, I could easily mark the difference in my life in many ways. Don't be mistaken: it goes without saying that my suffering, repentance, and transformation was far from over by the end of the night. It had only just begun, but I did have a deep and abiding faith in the process of mourning and redemptive transformation. One very big mark was how radically I saw the need for a sense of *urgency* to convey the message of the Gospel of Christ in any way I could.

Another mark was how I no longer hesitated to run toward the chaos in someone's life because I had seen how quickly one could and would shut the window blown open into their heart, not pausing long enough to peer inside and thereby missing a vital window of opportunity to change and be more like Christ.

Yet another mark was how vitally important it is to never write someone off as "too far gone" when they are, *like my father who I believe was converted, saved on Christmas night,* in a state of unconsciousness and apparently unreachable: God can and does speak and change a heart whenever he pleases. Judging anyone as "too far gone for God" is a crime of potentially eternal proportions. God's mercy is wider and deeper than we could imagine.

One of the important things I did not do well after Dad's tragic death was to spend time more fully reorienting myself to God, my family, and others who were about to be impacted by the radical changes that had occurred in my life. In many ways, I was a different person after that night in the garden. By not taking my own medicine, advice and the the time to mark the manifold changes that had occurred that night and the time that followed, I did a grave disservice to God, myself, and those around me.

When my wife, Peggy, and I were in counseling after Dad's death, the counselor once asked Peggy, "Have you mourned the death of the John you knew before his experience on Christmas night?"

Intriguing question, is it not? We need to mark the changes in concrete ways, or else our hearts will begin to turn back to stone—by suppressing the truth, conforming to the ways of this world; bowing to man and not God; staying silent about God's ways rather than speaking God's truth in love; becoming more and more lax about mortifying sin; becoming a consumer at church, not a member serving other; and all sorts of consequences related to the compartmentalization of our heart.

The Holy Spirit (wholeheartedly) intends changes wrought by redemptive suffering to propel us forward on the way to more authentic "word and deed and light and salt discipleship." We become near-fanatic, Christ-forwarding people, changed and challenged to pursue the next iteration of heart, spirit, faith, and story. God gives us an undaunted desire to reveal his glory to others—others whom he intends to convert and conform to the image of Christ. All people can be powerfully influenced by God and by your changed life.

Anytime we suffer, the way forward is the way described in the Bible, the way of Christ Jesus and his resurrection, of community impact and renewal. As we explore this in more depth, we should note that the believers described in the New Testament never directly asked God to remove the consequences of living in a broken world. This Gospel touchstone rooted in the reality of living in a world broken by mankind is vitally important to recall—and recoup. Rather, they asked that God, by means of the inevitable suffering, *would transform their hearts to more closely resemble Jesus's heart and then use them to bring the comfort of Christ to others* (Eph. 3; 2 Cor. 1:3–7; Phil. 2). Do you get this at a level that truly roots and motivates your life?

Don't forget, an enraged Satan is loose on the Earth (1 Pet. 5.8), and he intends to thwart Christ's cause in every way possible, using every method, weapon, and person at his disposal. He works to keep unbelievers from coming to faith. He works to make believers, those who already belong to Christ, as ineffective as possible in the Trinity's redemptive mission. Don't forget, don't be surprised, don't be neutered or drop-jawed stunned since sanctified suffering is a key to our growth and effectiveness, the deceiver and destroyer will oppose it at every turn!

Don't be surprised when a Christian brother or sister chooses to remain spiritually stunted. Don't be surprised by mass murder, government ineptness, statism, or corporate corruption. And don't let the surprise of sin paralyze you when it raises its ugly head in any individual or institution. Suffering will continue and escalate, until Christ comes again. *Transform your surprise into faith in action.* Run toward the chaos of this broken world, assure anyone in a free fall that God's foundations exist; once resting on the Rock of Ages solid assurance(s) of Creation, Christ, and Covenant; abide by the person at the blown-open window of their hearts to encourage growth in the Gospel; God and self-awareness, purification, holiness, and Christ-like conformation; and then help ready the person for the way forward—transformed by the partnership of the Spirit and our obedience, humbly, boldly, urgently and fully armored, faithfully moving into the chaos. Redeemed to redeem.

Because this is so, we join in Paul's ardent prayer for ourselves and for the hearts and spirits of other believers who, together with us, face life's battles. Together, we pray that all the sufferings we endure will bring about even more thorough sanctification and better works of righteousness.

*So I ask you not to lose heart over what I am suffering for you, which is your glory. For this reason I bow my knees before the Father, from whom every family in heaven and on earth is named, that according to the riches of his glory he may grant you to be strengthened with power through his Spirit in your inner being, SO THAT Christ may dwell in your hearts through faith—that you, being rooted and grounded in love, may have strength to comprehend with all the saints what is the breadth and length and height and depth, and to know the love of Christ that surpasses knowledge, that you may be filled with all the fullness of God.*
*(Eph. 3:13–21, caps added)*

The way forward involves moving out in faith with Christ and Christians, trusting our Redeemer King who has called us to work with him in sharing the good news of his redemption with our world. As his co-redeemers, we open ourselves to help and be hurt by others. Service involves suffering, which leads to further sanctification, which results in more Christ and more service. Get these four "principles and practices of the way" callings and God-pleasing, people-blessing concepts deep down into your heart:

1) Mark the change of heart: less stone, more flesh (Ezek. 11:17–21; 36).
2) Moan the purpose of the Spirit: less me, more Christ (Rom. 8:18–30).
3) Marvel the mercy of God: less whining, more worship (Rom. 11; 12:1–3).
4) Move the mountain with faith: less ruminating, more redeeming (Job 9; 19:25).

## 1. Mark the Change of Heart: Less Stone, More Flesh

Rebirth. Can you mark the period of time when your heart of stone was first regenerated by the Spirit and your conversion, repentance, and spiritual rebirth occurred? When and how were you born again (e.g., less stone, more flesh). Could you retell the story of your life and new life to others in ways that would (a) be appropriate to a particular person or audience, (b) glorify God, and (c) bless the listener?

Sanctification/Purification/Holiness. Following your conversion, can you mark the times of suffering (or joy) that resulted in a change or softening of your heart? Could you tell someone a story of God's glory and your growth in the refining fires of pain, loss, or heartbreak? Can you look at a hurting someone in the eyes, as your eyes well up with weeping, and comfort him or her in concrete ways you have been comforted by the Spirit? At the end of the day, can you—by knowing deep within doctrine and personal experience—unequivocally say, "Just as the Spirit did in the beginning,' ("The earth was without form and void, and darkness was over the face of the deep. And the Spirit of God was hovering over the face of the waters." Gen. 1:2) he does so over my heart and yours today. *Mark the change of heart: less stone, more flesh?*"

## 2. Moan the Purpose of the Spirit: Less Me, More Christ

Do you believe it—having experienced it—that "the good" in "for those who love God all things work together for good, for those who are called according to his purpose" (Rom. 8:28) is all about "Less me, more Christ"? Can you say—whether "all things" are heartbreak or joy—God, by the Spirit, is working on your behalf to conform you more and more into the likeness of Jesus Christ? "I trust in the whole and holistic work of the Trinity on my behalf to work any and all levels of pain and or pleasure for the good of making me more like Christ." Does that testimony fit (even remotely or completely) well within your story, heart, and hope for others? How closely do you feel in your knowledge of and relationship with the Holy Spirit, God in residence in your heart (John 14:16, 26; 2 Cor. 1:22)? Consider praying to the effect of being much closer to the Spirit and his role and goal as your Counselor, Pointer to Jesus, Supernatural Heart Changer—all for the purpose of "Less you, more Christ."

## 3. Marvel the Mercy of God: Less Whining, More Worship

Can you describe some milestones along the journey of your faith that make you marvel at God's person, power, and practical forms of blessing you? If so, there's a very good likelihood you're not much into whining, grumbling, and complaining about God and life, right? In fact, have you seen how *marveling* and *whining* cannot coexist? If you've had a Spirit-inspired desire to ramp up the marvel you have about God—Father, Son, Holy Spirit—what measures would you be willing to take to cultivate this worthy appetite? Are you self-aware and honest enough to see when and why whining, grumbling, and complaining got the better of you, and how you could sense the signs of idolatry, mortify the sin, hard-heartedness, and nip it in the bud?

## 4. Move the Mountain with Faith: Less Ruminating, More Redeeming

Seen from the thirty-thousand foot level, the book of Job takes into account God's allowing Satan and the brokenness of this world to tear Job's—a faithful man of God—heart, family, health, belongings, and entire life to pieces. The story is mostly comprised of ruminating, brainstorming, brooding, meditating, pondering, cogitating, and endless deliberating about God and suffering. The story ends after thirty-seven chapters (count 'em: thirty-seven!) of the above. Then God himself intercedes: "I am God; you are not. Now we can begin to relate to one another" (Job 38–41). But Job's refined and more holy faith (as a result of severe suffering) bore the fruit of a profound, universal yet personal declaration during the suffering, "For I know that my Redeemer lives, and at the last he will stand upon the earth!" (Job 19:25). Can you say this along with Job with full-hearted conviction?

When someone—anyone—asks you what you know about a substantive issue, can you, will you respond in like fashion: "Well, honestly, the most important thing is I know my Redeemer lives and I have been redeemed to redeem"? In regards to the issue at hand, and after reading this book this far, where does the question "How could an all-powerful and all-loving God allow such horrid and widespread suffering in the world?" sit with you now? Can you answer it first for yourself and then for another person? Or are you still prone to ruminating, brainstorming, brooding, meditating, pondering, etc. about this vitally important question of theodicy (e.g., the branch of theology that defends God's goodness and justice in the face of the existence of evil)? Do you envision yourself as "less ruminating, more redeeming?"

Bless it forward. Even though there are many different ways to express your faith or provide an apologetic for the story and defense of your Christian walk to a watching, wounded, and wandering world, can you say of yourself you've been redeemed to redeem, comforted to comfort, loved by Jesus Christ to love others, rescued to rescue, saved to help save others, or whatever form of expressing God's plan of the world's redemption in yourself? If you are a born-again Christian (which is the only kind), this is the main reason God has given you life "today" (Ps. 95:7–8).

So again the question, "How can an all-powerful and all-loving God allow such horrid and widespread suffering in the world?" While there are certainly mysteries, there is no mystery that is sufficient for God's people not to act in faith and help redeem, or transform the world. As we have seen in my story, and just one of many worthy explanations of God and suffering, God has revealed more than enough of his powerful truth, love, and plan of redemption. We just have to remember, reinvigorate, and refresh ourselves "today."

## Mark, Moan, Marvel, Move...This!

As we have seen, God does not cause our suffering (mankind did), but he will sovereignly and most mercifully orchestrate and *use* our suffering to draw us closer to him for the purposes of being made more like his Son and to "go out into all the world" (Matt. 28:16–20). We have been given the blessing of free will—love is not love unless it's freely reciprocated. We know suffering happens because of Adam's Original Sin that brings death on earth, and to all of us. But also we know there is a saving grace in trusting Jesus Christ as Savior (from Hell) and Lord (of our life). Keenly aware of the *ideal*, we exemplify Christ in the *real*, knowing full well the gap between the two (ideal and real) will be forever closed when Christ returns to make all things new. What a glory and consummation to God's story that will be—but not yet.

I believe there has never been a greater need for human beings to understand the "anatomy of the heart" as God so universally, personally, and carefully created it; to consider the ways in which human hearts have been impacted by the fall into sin; and to use the unique, ingenious, and specific plan God has provided for not only putting the heart back together again—not in a Humpty-Dumpty, Elmer's Glue-All way—but refashioning, refurbishing, and redeeming it for far, far greater purposes than we could ever (in a gazillion years) imagine or hope for, beloved.

### *"Above all else, guard your heart, for it is—it really and truly is—the wellspring of life" (Prov. 4:23, emphasis added).*

The weeping, the window, and the way. The way is transformative and timely in what's needed to revolutionize the church. Please remember the original and this boiled-down version of my book is written first to "Christians living in a culture of comfort" who have gotten too comfy for God and our "alien-stranger" nature and mission. The body of Christ is where the heart change first needs to occur. Then and only then can a watching and not-surprisingly, justifiably skeptical world begin to have an explanation and example of real-life redemptive suffering: the fuller, more complete weight of God's protocol for redemptive suffering will be seen in *time* as well as the promise of transformation that will be evident in and for *eternity*. Heaven, the Judgment Seat of Christ, is a place where rewards will be given or lost, depending on how a believer has lived his life for the Lord (1 Thess. 2:19–20) and, as an additional spin on this promise, how a believer has lived his life for the Lord in the midst of unavoidable, sanctifying suffering.

Don't miss this: how we have stewarded God's plan for redemptive suffering now will be as plain as the makeup and stature of our new selves in Heaven then. Greater maturity and impact on earth will result in greater rewards and stature in Heaven. And not just for ourselves (Rom. 15:1).

## Take Heart, Take Hope, but Take Note

"Therefore I intend always to remind you" (2 Pet. 12). You know there's a battle going on, right? The battle for us to believe, internalize, and live out any or all of the above truisms of the born-again heart, spirit, and life on mission for Christ. This is a three-against-one glorious and gory battle. Christ has won the war, but the battle, the life-and-death skirmishes are not over, and the carnage is still very real and widespread.

The three-against-one battle consists of the world, the flesh, and the devil against Christ—in the Body of Christ (the church supernatural], bona fide born-again Christians anywhere, and the church institutional. Know your enemy well! Like any wise leader involved in a battle for his life and the lives of his soldiers, not knowing the enemy is a losing proposition. Be acutely aware and wise about this triple threat: (a) the ways of this world (1 John 2:15–17; Rom. 12:2; Col. 3:2, and many more); (b) the flesh (Rom. 8:8; 1 Cor. 6:18; Gal. 5:17, and many more); and (c) the Devil (1 Pet. 5:8; James 4:7; Eph. 6:11–12; John 8:44, and many more).

You can be sure of this: this trifecta of darkness has promised and is poised to diminish the spiritual, emotional, psychological/ mental, and physical impact of God's protocol for redemptive suffering. Don't forget, the realms of darkness are committed to keeping unbelievers from believing and believers from being effective. *And wasting our tears is a very big and all-too-popular temptation that makes any Christian far less effective than God hopes for and our hearts deeply desire.*

## TAKE HEART

*The Heart Combating the World, the Flesh, and the Devil: The converted heart of the Christian will war against the world's ways, the flesh ["the old man," remaining sin], and the Devil until Jesus returns to make all things new. Christian, be wise, and put on the armor!*

Never has there been a more appropriate time to engage near-fanatic urgency to deal in wisdom and in community with the things of the heart—its origins, its fall, its temporal and eternal redemption—and to develop a systematic action plan for doing so continually in everyday life. As the New Testament author Paul writes to the Church at Philippi in Philippians 2, when you and I choose better over bitter, the overflow of God's redemptive love will absolutely be used to redeem and refresh others as well. The comfort God has in store for you is so (never more so) needed in the world today.

## Don't Be Surprised, Consider It All Joy: The Cycle of Suffering until Jesus Returns—It Will Make an Eternity of Difference

The cycle of redemptive suffering—exemplified by the weeping, the window, and the way—is something the first-century Bible writers repeatedly reminded and admonished the worldly, surprised, and frightened Christians about. Please check out the cycle and how it repeats itself in the life ascending—over and over, higher and higher, more and more like Jesus, until he comes again in glory and we see him face to face. Did you know, have you deeply, closely considered that how well or wastefully you steward your suffering will be evidenced in heaven for eternity? Your character, your stature, your station, your rewards, even the detailed lines of beautification seen in your face will be a reflection of how faithfully you and I applied "God's protocol for redemptive suffering"—seen in this version of it or in other biblically consistent forms (1 Cor. 4:5; 2 Cor. 5:10). Steward your suffering well, beloved.

***Beloved, do not be surprised at the fiery ordeal among you, which comes upon you for your testing, as though some strange thing were happening to you; but to the degree that you share the sufferings of Christ, keep on rejoicing, so that also at the revelation of his glory you may rejoice with exultation. (1 Pet. 4:12–13; James 1:1; Rom. 5:3–5)***

*JOHN O. DOZIER, JR.*

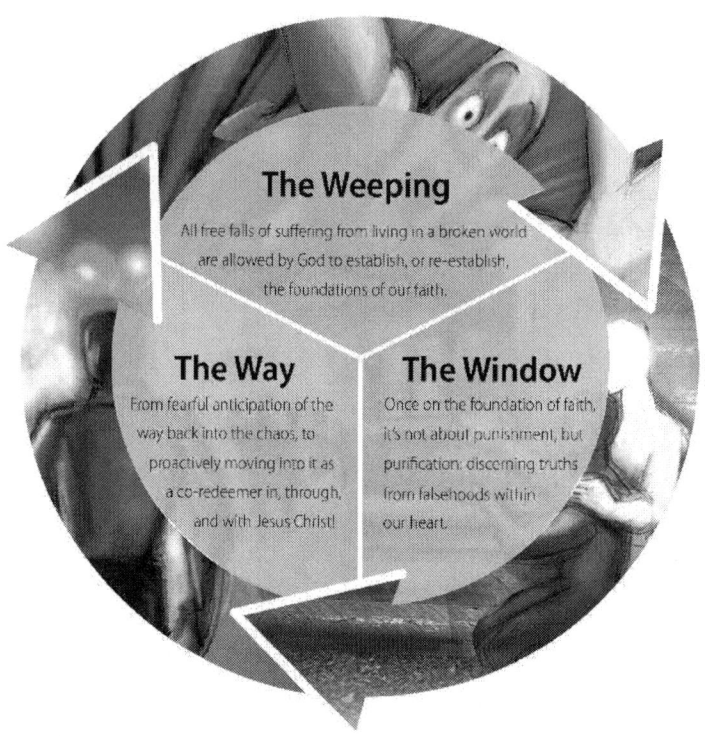

*The Cycle of Redemptive Suffering: The brokenness of this world will remain unabated until Christ returns, but the far, far greater glory of the Saints being more and more conformed to the image of Christ is worth all the praise and practice we can imagine. That's why Christians proclaim, "Consider it all joy..." (James 1:1)!*

*TAKE HEART*

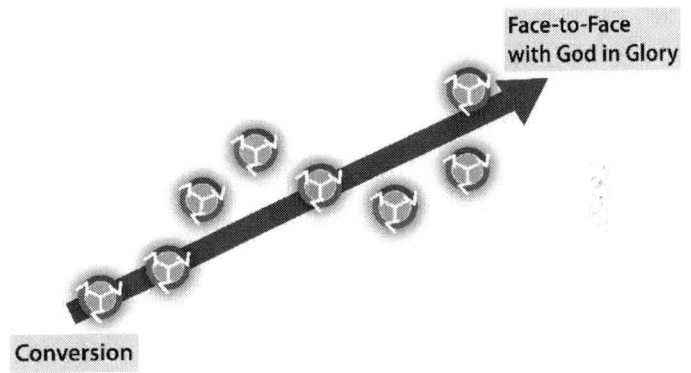

*The Weeping, Window, Way Ascending to Glory! The Cycle of Redemptive Suffering happens; it has its ups and downs; but knowing, experiencing that becoming more and more like Jesus Christ until we stand face-to-face with him is an ascending journey of hope and glory; it's essential to remember each and every day!*

*JOHN O. DOZIER, JR.*

# Christian, Get Your "So That" Deep: The God of All Comfort Comforts "So That"

*Blessed be the God and Father of our Lord Jesus Christ, the Father of mercies and God of all comfort, who comforts us in all our affliction, SO THAT we may be able to comfort those who are in any affliction, with the comfort with which we ourselves are comforted by God. For as we share abundantly in Christ's sufferings, so through Christ we share abundantly in comfort too.
(2 Cor. 1:3–5, emphasis added; Phil. 2:1–11)*

## A Bird's-Eye Before We End

Since folks are so busy and distracted these days, here's a bird's-eye view you can hang onto now, throughout our journey together, and beyond—until you see the earmarks of this truth in who you are for eternity:

1) The Weeping: In a broken world where suffering is unavoidable, all pain, trials, or "the free falls of life" are providentially-allowed by God for the purposes of reminding us to see what the foundations of our life consist of—Creation, Christ, and Covenant… or some faulty set of beliefs, idols, vanities, or misconceptions. Trials are used of God as tests of our foundational beliefs.

2) The Window: In Christ, once we're reminded of the fact that we're resting on the unshakable foundations of God's Creation, Christ, and Covenant, we can see the suffering is not about

punishment, but purification: We're invited to take whatever time it takes to spend time looking into the window of our heart to discern the truths and falsehood that we hold dear inside our heart—the repository of our faith. This "window of heart cleansing" won't stay open for long... Do not waste your heartbreak!

3) The Way: Before we turn back to face and help redeem the chaos of this broken world as changed, conformed, co-redeemers in Christ, we must get some very important things straight. As we will see, it's about Marking. Moaning. Marveling. And Moving—before we turn and intentionally walk into the chaos of brokenness where we're called to be Christ's claim, comfort, and compassion.

In short, God's consolation "Take Heart, Beloved!", and perfect plan for your pain, is captured in The Weeping, the Window, and the Way.

*Dearest Reader,*
*This book is a plea, an unabashed entreaty to allow the God of the universe to meet you in your pain, to transform you through your pain.*
*Amen.*

# "The Weeping, the Window, the Way" Bible Chapter-Verse Reference

*References that are inordinately long are not referenced below.*

**All Scripture is breathed out by God and profitable for teaching, for reproof, for correction, and for training in righteousness, that the man of God may be complete, equipped for every good work.
(2 Tim. 3:16)**

## Chapter One: The Christmas Crèche and Heartbreaking Crisis

Genesis 3

John 3:16—For God so loved the world, that he gave his only Son, that whoever believes in him should not perish but have eternal life.

1 John 1:9—If we confess our sins, he is faithful and just to forgive us our sins and to cleanse us from all unrighteousness.

Genesis 1:21—And God saw everything that he had made, and behold, it was very good. And there was evening and there was morning, the sixth day.

Revelation 21:1–5—Then I saw a new heaven and a new earth, for the first heaven and the first earth had passed away, and the sea was no more. And I saw the holy city, new Jerusalem, coming down out of heaven from God, prepared as a bride adorned for her husband. And I heard a loud voice from the throne saying, "Behold, the dwelling place of God is with man. He will dwell with them, and they will be his people, and God himself will be with them as their God. He will wipe away every tear from their eyes, and death shall be no more, neither shall there be mourning, nor crying, nor pain anymore, for the former things have passed away." And he who was seated on the throne said, "Behold, I am making all things new."

Revelation 22:12—Behold, I am coming soon, bringing my recompense with me, to repay each one for what he has done.

Genesis 1:1—In the beginning, God created the heavens and the earth.

Genesis 1:26–27—Then God said, "Let us make man in our image, after our likeness. And let them have dominion over the fish of the sea and over the birds of the heavens and over the livestock and over all the earth and over every creeping thing that creeps on the earth." So God created man in his own image, in the image of God he created him; male and female he created them.

Genesis 2:7—then the LORD God formed the man of dust from the ground and breathed into his nostrils the breath of life, and the man became a living creature.

## *TAKE HEART*

Genesis 3

Psalm 51:5—Behold, I was brought forth in iniquity, and in sin did my mother conceive me.

Genesis 2:17—but the tree of knowledge of good and evil you shall not eat, for in the day that you eat of it you will surely die

Romans 1:18–32—Look this one up! Key passage on sin.

Ephesians 4:19—They have become callous and have given themselves up to sensuality, greedy to practice every kind of impurity.

2 Peter 2:14—They have eyes full of adultery, insatiable for sin. They entice unsteady souls. They have hearts trained in greed. Accursed children!

Leviticus 26:30—And I will destroy your high places and cut down your incense altars and cast your dead bodies upon the dead bodies of your idols, and my soul will abhor you.

Deuteronomy 30:17—But if your heart turns away, and you will not hear, but are drawn away to worship other gods and serve them...

Exodus 20:1–7—And God spoke all these words, saying, "I am the Lord your God, who brought you out of the land of Egypt, out of the house of slavery. "You shall have no other gods before[a] me. "You shall not make for yourself a carved image, or any likeness of anything that is in heaven above, or that is in the earth beneath, or that is in the water under the earth. You shall not bow down to them or serve them, for I the Lord your God am a jealous God, visiting the iniquity of the fathers on the children to the third and the fourth generation of those who hate me, but showing steadfast love to thousands of those who love me and keep my commandments. "You shall not take the name of the Lord your God in vain, for the Lord will not hold him guiltless who takes his name in vain."

Ezekiel 11:21—But as for those whose heart goes after their detestable things and their abominations, I will bring their deeds upon their own heads, declares the Lord God."

Luke 16:15—And he said to them, "You are those who justify yourselves before men, but God knows your hearts. For what is exalted among men is an abomination in the sight of God."

2 Thessalonians 3:5—May the Lord direct your hearts to the love of God and to the steadfastness of Christ.

Jeremiah 9:26—Egypt, Judah, Edom, the sons of Ammon, Moab, and all who dwell in the desert who cut the corners of their hair, for all these nations are uncircumcised, and all the house of Israel are uncircumcised in heart.

Ezekiel 44:7—in admitting foreigners, uncircumcised in heart and flesh, to be in my sanctuary, profaning my temple, when you offer to me my food, the fat and the blood. You have broken my covenant, in addition to all your abominations.

Acts 7:51—You stiff-necked people, uncircumcised in heart and ears, you always resist the Holy Spirit. As your fathers did, so do you.

## TAKE HEART

Exodus 4:21—And the Lord said to Moses, "When you go back to Egypt, see that you do before Pharaoh all the miracles that I have put in your power. But I will harden his heart, so that he will not let the people go."

Proverbs 26:23—Like the glaze covering an earthen vessel are fervent lips with an evil heart.

Proverbs 11:20—Those of crooked heart are an abomination to the Lord, but those of blameless ways are his delight.

Job 36:13—The godless in heart cherish anger; they do not cry for help when he binds them.

Romans 7:15–20—For I do not understand my own actions. For I do not do what I want, but I do the very thing I hate. Now if I do what I do not want, I agree with the law, that it is good. So now it is no longer I who do it, but sin that dwells within me. For I know that nothing good dwells in me, that is, in my flesh. For I have the desire to do what is right, but not the ability to carry it out. For I do not do the good I want, but the evil I do not want is what I keep on doing. Now if I do what I do not want, it is no longer I who do it, but sin that dwells within me.

Romans 8:37—No, in all things we are more than conquerors through him who loved us.

## Chapter Two: We Can't Hear God's Protocol for Redemptive Suffering Enough

John 19:30—When Jesus had received the sour wine, he said, "it is finished," and he bowed his head and gave up his spirit.

Colossians 1:26—The mystery hidden for ages and generations but now is revealed to his saints.

Revelation 21:5—and he who was seated on the throne said, "behold, I am making all things new." Also he said, "Write this down, for these words are trustworthy and true."

2 Corinthians 5:17—Therefore, if anyone is in Christ, he is a new creation. The old has passed away; behold, the new has come.

Galatians 3:26—For in Christ Jesus you are all sons of God, through faith.

1 John 5:11–12—And this is the testimony, that God gave us eternal life, and this life is in his son. Whoever has the son has life; whoever does not have the son does not have life.

John 3:3—Jesus answered him, "Truly, truly, I say unto you, unless one is born again he cannot see the kingdom of God."

Romans 1:18–32—God's wrath on unrighteousness. It's longer, but look this one up!

## *TAKE HEART*

Ephesians 2:8–9—For by grace you have been saved through faith. And this is not of your own doing; it is the gift of God, not a result of works, so that no one may boast.

Ephesians 1:4–5—Even as he chose us in him before the foundation of the world, that we should be holy and blameless before him. In love he predestined us for adoption as sons through Christ Jesus, according to the purpose of his will.

Acts 3:19—Repent therefore, and turned back, that your sins may be blotted out.

Acts 2:38—And Peter said to them, "Repent and be baptized every one of you in the name of Jesus Christ for the forgiveness of your sins, and you will receive the gift of the Holy Spirit."

John 3:3—Jesus answered him, "Truly, truly, I say to you, unless one is born again he cannot see the kingdom of God."

Galatians 2:20—I have been crucified with Christ. It is no longer I who live, but Christ to lives in me. And the life I now live in the flesh I live by faith in the son of God, who loved me and gave himself for me.

Hebrews 11:6—And without faith it is impossible to please God, for whoever would draw near to God must believe that he exists and that he rewards those who seek him.

Psalm 95:7–8—For he is our God, and we are the people of his pasture, and the sheep of his hand. Today, if you hear his voice, do not harden your hearts, as at Meribah, as on the day at Massah in the wilderness,

2 Corinthians 6:2—For he says, "In a favorable time I listened to you, and in a day of salvation I have helped you." Behold, now is the favorable time; behold, now is the day of salvation.

Ephesians 2:1–10—And you were dead in the trespasses and sins 2 in which you once walked, following the course of this world, following the prince of the power of the air, the spirit that is now at work in the sons of disobedience—among whom we all once lived in the passions of our flesh, carrying out the desires of the body and the mind, and were by nature children of wrath, like the rest of mankind. But God, being rich in mercy, because of the great love with which he loved us, even when we were dead in our trespasses, made us alive together with Christ—by grace you have been saved—and raised us up with him and seated us with him in the heavenly places in Christ Jesus, so that in the coming ages he might show the immeasurable riches of his grace in kindness toward us in Christ Jesus. For by grace you have been saved through faith. And this is not your own doing; it is the gift of God, not a result of works, so that no one may boast. For we are his workmanship, created in Christ Jesus for good works, which God prepared beforehand, that we should walk in them.

Romans 8:28—And we know that for those who love God all things work together for good, for those who are called according to his purpose.

## TAKE HEART

James 1:2–4—Count it all joy, my brothers,[a] when you meet trials of various kinds, for you know that the testing of your faith produces steadfastness. And let steadfastness have its full effect, that you may be perfect and complete, lacking in nothing.

Exodus 20

Matthew 22:34–40—But when the Pharisees heard that he had silenced the Sadducees, they gathered together. And one of them, a lawyer, asked him a question to test him. "Teacher, which is the great commandment in the Law?" And he said to him, "You shall love the Lord your God with all your heart and with all your soul and with all your mind. This is the great and first commandment. And a second is like it: You shall love your neighbor as yourself. On these two commandments depend all the Law and the Prophets."

2 Corinthians 1:3–7—Blessed be the God and Father of our Lord Jesus Christ, the Father of mercies and God of all comfort, who comforts us in all our affliction, so that we may be able to comfort those who are in any affliction, with the comfort with which we ourselves are comforted by God. 5 For as we share abundantly in Christ's sufferings, so through Christ we share abundantly in comfort too. If we are afflicted, it is for your comfort and salvation; and if we are comforted, it is for your comfort, which you experience when you patiently endure the same sufferings that we suffer. 7 Our hope for you is unshaken, for we know that as you share in our sufferings, you will also share in our comfort.

Hebrews 11:6—And without faith it is impossible to please him, for whoever would draw near to God must believe that he exists and that he rewards those who seek him.

John 8:24—I told you that you would die in your sins, for unless you believe that I am he you will die in your sins.

Joshua 24:15—And if it is evil in your eyes to serve the LORD, choose this day whom you will serve, whether the gods your fathers served in the region beyond the River, or the gods of the Amorites in whose land you dwell. But as for me and my house, we will serve the LORD.

## Chapter Three: Living in a Culture of Comfort

Acts 5:29—But Peter and the apostles answered, "We must obey God rather than men."

1 Peter 1:14—As obedient children, do not be conformed to the passions of your former ignorance

Luke 12:22–31—And he said to his disciples, "Therefore I tell you, do not be anxious about your life, what you will eat, nor about your body, what you will put on. 23 For life is more than food, and the body more than clothing. 24 Consider the ravens: they neither sow nor reap, they have neither storehouse nor barn, and yet God feeds them. Of how much more value are you than the birds! 25 And which of you by being anxious can add a single hour to his span of life? 26 If then you are not able to do as small a thing as that, why are you anxious about the rest? 27 Consider the lilies, how they grow: they neither toil nor spin, yet I tell you, even Solomon in all his glory was not arrayed like one of these. 28 But if God so clothes the grass, which is alive in the field today, and tomorrow is thrown into the oven, how much more will he clothe you, O you of little faith! 29 And do not seek what you are to eat and what you are to drink, nor be worried. 30 For all the nations of the world seek after these things, and your Father knows that you need them. 31 Instead, seek his kingdom, and these things will be added to you.

Genesis 1:31—And God saw everything that he had made, and behold, it was very good. And there was evening and there was morning, the sixth day.

## Chapter Four: Take Heart

1 Samuel 13:13–14—And Samuel said to Saul, "You have done foolishly. You have not kept the command of the Lord your God, with which he commanded you. For then the Lord would have established your kingdom over Israel forever. But now your kingdom shall not continue. The Lord has sought out a man after his own heart, and the Lord has commanded him to be prince[a] over his people, because you have not kept what the Lord commanded you."

Luke 10:27—And he answered, "You shall love the Lord your God with all your heart and with all your soul and with all your strength and with all your mind, and your neighbor as yourself."

Galatians 5:22–23—But the fruit of the Spirit is love, joy, peace, patience, kindness, goodness, faithfulness, 23 gentleness, self-control; against such things there is no law.

Galatians 5:19–21—Now the works of the flesh are evident: sexual immorality, impurity, sensuality, 20 idolatry, sorcery, enmity, strife, jealousy, fits of anger, rivalries, dissensions, divisions, 21 envy, drunkenness, orgies, and things like these. I warn you, as I warned you before, that those who do such things will not inherit the kingdom of God.

Mark 16:16—Whoever believes and is baptized will be saved, but whoever does not believe will be condemned.

Revelation 3:16—So, because you are lukewarm, and neither hot nor cold, I will spit you out of my mouth.

Psalm 30

Psalm 119:71—It is good for me that I was afflicted, that I might learn your statutes.

2 Corinthians 12:5—On behalf of this man I will boast, but on my own behalf I will not boast, except of my weaknesses.

2 Corinthians 12:9–10—But he said to me, "My grace is sufficient for you, for my power is made perfect in weakness." Therefore I will boast all the more gladly of my weaknesses, so that the power of Christ may rest upon me. For the sake of Christ, then, I am content with weaknesses, insults, hardships, persecutions, and calamities. For when I am weak, then I am strong.

## TAKE HEART

Romans 5

Hebrews 1

Proverbs 3:11–12—My son, do not despise the LORD's discipline or be weary of his reproof, for the LORD reproves him whom he loves, as a father the son in whom he delights.

John 17:17—[Jesus praying to God the Father] Sanctify them in the truth; your word is truth.

Romans 8:28—And we know that for those who love God all things work together for good for those who are called according to his purpose.

1 Corinthians 11:32—But when we are judged by the Lord, we are disciplined so that we may not be condemned along with the world.

Hebrews 12:8—If you are left without discipline, in which all have participated, then you are illegitimate children and not sons.

Hebrews 13:12—So Jesus also suffered outside the gate in order to sanctify the people through his own blood.

2 Corinthians 3:18—And we all, with unveiled face, beholding the glory of the Lord, are being transformed into the same image from one degree of glory to another. For this comes from the Lord who is the Spirit.

Romans 8:29—For those whom he foreknew he also predestined to be conformed to the image of his Son, in order that he might be the firstborn among many brothers.

Romans 12:2—Do not be conformed to this world, but be transformed by the renewal of your mind, that by testing you may discern what is the will of God, what is good and acceptable and perfect.

Hebrews 2:10—For it was fitting that he, for whom and by whom all things exist, in bringing many sons to glory, should make the founder of their salvation perfect through suffering.

Romans 11:33–34—Oh, the depth of the riches and wisdom and knowledge of God! How unsearchable are his judgments and how inscrutable his ways! "For who has known the mind of the Lord, or who has been his counselor?"

James 1

Colossians 1:24—Now I rejoice in my sufferings for your sake, and in my flesh I am filling up what is lacking in Christ's afflictions for the sake of his body, that is, the church.

Psalm 72:12—For he delivers the needy when he calls, the poor and him who has no helper.

2 Corinthians 1:3-7—Blessed be the God and Father of our Lord Jesus Christ, the Father of mercies and God of all comfort, who comforts us in all our affliction, so that we may be able to comfort those who are in any affliction, with the comfort with which we ourselves are comforted by God. For as we share abundantly in Christ's sufferings, so through Christ we share abundantly in comfort too. If we are afflicted, it is for your comfort and salvation; and if

we are comforted, it is for your comfort, which you experience when you patiently endure the same sufferings that we suffer. Our hope for you is unshaken, for we know that as you share in our sufferings, you will also share in our comfort.

James 1:27—Religion that is pure and undefiled before God, the Father, is this: to visit orphans and widows in their affliction, and to keep oneself unstained from the world.

Matthew 3:8—Bear fruit in keeping with repentance.

John 12:24—Truly, truly, I say to you, unless a grain of wheat falls into the earth and dies, it remains alone; but if it dies, it bears much fruit.

Galatians 5

Ezekiel 11:18–21—And when they come there, they will remove from it all its detestable things and all its abominations. And I will give them one heart, and a new spirit I will put within them. I will remove the heart of stone from their flesh and give them a heart of flesh, that they may walk in my statutes and keep my rules and obey them. And they shall be my people, and I will be their God. But as for those whose heart goes after their detestable things and their abominations, I will bring their deeds upon their own heads, declares the Lord GOD."

Luke 24:26—Was it not necessary that the Christ should suffer these things and enter into his glory?"

2 Corinthians 1:5—For as we share abundantly in Christ's sufferings, so through Christ we share abundantly in comfort too.

Philippians 3:8—Indeed, I count everything as loss because of the surpassing worth of knowing Christ Jesus my Lord. For his sake I have suffered the loss of all things and count them as rubbish, in order that I may gain Christ

1 Peter 5

Psalm 39:6—Surely a man goes about as a shadow! Surely for nothing they are in turmoil; man heaps up wealth and does not know who will gather!

1 Corinthians 7:31—and those who deal with the world as though they had no dealings with it. For the present form of this world is passing away.

2 Corinthians 12:7—So to keep me from becoming conceited because of the surpassing greatness of the revelations, a thorn was given me in the flesh, a messenger of Satan to harass me, to keep me from becoming conceited.

1 Peter 1:24—For "All flesh is like grass and all its glory like the flower of grass. The grass withers, and the flower falls."

Genesis 48:4—(Jacob telling his son Joseph just before Jacob died what God had said to him.) And [God Almighty] said to me, "Behold, I will make you fruitful and multiply you, and I will make of you a company of peoples and will give this land to your offspring after you for an everlasting possession."

Hebrews 13

Romans 1:12—that is, that we may be mutually encouraged by each other's faith, both yours and mine.

Colossians 2:2—that their hearts may be encouraged, being knit together in love, to reach all the riches of full assurance of understanding and the knowledge of God's mystery, which is Christ.

Galatians 6:2—Bear one another's burdens, and so fulfill the law of Christ.

Jeremiah 29:11—For I know the plans I have for you, declares the LORD, plans for welfare and not for evil, to give you a future and a hope.

Romans 5:2–5—Through him we have also obtained access by faith into this grace in which we stand, and we rejoice in hope of the glory of God. 3 Not only that, but we rejoice in our sufferings, knowing that suffering produces endurance, 4 and endurance produces character, and character produces hope, 5 and hope does not put us to shame, because God's love has been poured into our hearts through the Holy Spirit who has been given to us.

Romans 15:1—We who are strong have an obligation to bear with the failings of the weak, and not to please ourselves.

2 Corinthians 1:3–7—Blessed be the God and Father of our Lord Jesus Christ, the Father of mercies and God of

all comfort, 4 who comforts us in all our affliction, so that we may be able to comfort those who are in any affliction, with the comfort with which we ourselves are comforted by God. 5 For as we share abundantly in Christ's sufferings, so through Christ we share abundantly in comfort too. 6 If we are afflicted, it is for your comfort and salvation; and if we are comforted, it is for your comfort, which you experience when you patiently endure the same sufferings that we suffer. 7 Our hope for you is unshaken, for we know that as you share in our sufferings, you will also share in our comfort.

Philippians 2

## Chapter Five: The Weeping: Free Falls and Foundations

Ezekiel 11:19—And I will give them one heart, and a new spirit I will put within them. I will remove the heart of stone from their flesh and give them a heart of flesh,

Jeremiah 24:7—I will give them a heart to know that I am the LORD, and they shall be my people and I will be their God, for they shall return to me with their whole heart.

Matthew 22:37—And he [Jesus] said to him, "You shall love the Lord your God with all your heart and with all your soul and with all your mind."

2 Corinthians 5:17—Therefore, if anyone is in Christ, he is a new creation. The old has passed away; behold, the new has come.

John 3:16—For God so loved the world, that he gave his only Son, that whoever believes in him should not perish but have eternal life.

2 Corinthians 1:3–7—Blessed be the God and Father of our Lord Jesus Christ, the Father of mercies and God of all comfort, 4 who comforts us in all our affliction, so that we may be able to comfort those who are in any affliction, with the comfort with which we ourselves are comforted by God. 5 For as we share abundantly in Christ's sufferings, so through Christ we share abundantly in comfort too. 6 If we are afflicted, it is for your comfort and salvation; and if we are comforted, it is for your comfort, which you experience when you patiently endure the same sufferings that we suffer. 7 Our hope for you is unshaken, for we know that as you share in our sufferings, you will also share in our comfort.

## Chapter Six: The Window: Fallen, Forgiven, Free

Psalm 95:7–8—For he is our God, and we are the people of his pasture, and the sheep of his hand. Today, if you hear his voice, do not harden your hearts, as at Meribah, as on the day at Massah in the wilderness,

Ezekiel 11, 36

John 3:3—Jesus answered him, "Truly, truly, I say to you, unless one is born again he cannot see the kingdom of God."

2 Corinthians 5:17—Therefore, if anyone is in Christ, he is a new creation. The old has passed away; behold, the new has come.

John 17

Romans 6:5–6—For if we have been united with him in a death like his, we shall certainly be united with him in a resurrection like his. 6 We know that our old self was crucified with him in order that the body of sin might be brought to nothing, so that we would no longer be enslaved to sin.

2 Corinthians 4:7–18—But we have this treasure in jars of clay, to show that the surpassing power belongs to God and not to us. 8 We are afflicted in every way, but not crushed; perplexed, but not driven to despair; 9 persecuted, but not forsaken; struck down, but not destroyed; 10 always carrying in the body the death of Jesus, so that the life of Jesus may also be manifested in our bodies. 11 For we who live are always being given over to death for Jesus' sake, so that the life of Jesus also may be manifested in our mortal flesh. 12 So death is at work in us, but life in you.

13 Since we have the same spirit of faith according to what has been written, "I believed, and so I spoke," we also believe, and so we also speak, 14 knowing that he who raised the Lord Jesus will raise us also with Jesus and bring us with you into his presence. 15 For it is all for your sake, so that as grace extends to more and more people it may increase thanksgiving, to the glory of God.

## *TAKE HEART*

16 So we do not lose heart. Though our outer self is wasting away, our inner self is being renewed day by day. 17 For this light momentary affliction is preparing for us an eternal weight of glory beyond all comparison, 18 as we look not to the things that are seen but to the things that are unseen. For the things that are seen are transient, but the things that are unseen are eternal.

James 1:2–4—Count it all joy, my brothers,[a] when you meet trials of various kinds, 3 for you know that the testing of your faith produces steadfastness. And let steadfastness have its full effect, that you may be perfect and complete, lacking in nothing.

Ezekiel 11:19—And I will give them one heart, and a new spirit I will put within them. I will remove the heart of stone from their flesh and give them a heart of flesh.

Ezekiel 36:26—And I will give you a new heart, and a new spirit I will put within you. And I will remove the heart of stone from your flesh and give you a heart of flesh.

2 Timothy 2:21—Therefore, if anyone cleanses himself from what is dishonorable, he will be a vessel for honorable use, set apart as holy, useful to the master of the house, ready for every good work.

John 17:17—Sanctify them in the truth; your word is truth.

1 Peter 1:12—It was revealed to them that they were serving not themselves but you, in the things that have now been announced to you through those who preached the good news to you by the Holy Spirit sent from heaven, things into which angels long to look.

Mark 16:16—Whoever believes and is baptized will be saved, but whoever does not believe will be condemned.

Romans 7

Romans 10:9—because, if you confess with your mouth that Jesus is Lord and believe in your heart that God raised him from the dead, you will be saved.

Ephesians 1

Proverbs 4:23—Keep your heart with all vigilance, for from it flow the springs of life.

John 17:21—that they may all be one, just as you, Father, are in me, and I in you, that they also may be in us, so that the world may believe that you have sent me.

Romans 8:28–29—And we know that for those who love God all things work together for good, for those who are called according to his purpose. 29 For those whom he foreknew he also predestined to be conformed to the image of his Son, in order that he might be the firstborn among many brothers.

1 John 1:9—If we confess our sins, he is faithful and just to forgive us our sins and to cleanse us from all unrighteousness.

Jeremiah 2—(Take the time to read this chapter.)

James 4:4—You adulterous people! Do you not know that friendship with the world is enmity with God? Therefore whoever wishes to be a friend of the world makes himself an enemy of God.

# TAKE HEART

1 John 2:15–17—Do not love the world or the things in the world. If anyone loves the world, the love of the Father is not in him. For all that is in the world—the desires of the flesh and the desires of the eyes and pride of life—is not from the Father but is from the world. And the world is passing away along with its desires, but whoever does the will of God abides forever.

## Chapter Seven: The Way: Bringing Our Transformed Hearts Back into the Chaos

1 Corinthians 3:13—Each one's work will become manifest, for the Day will disclose it, because it will be revealed by fire, and the fire will test what sort of work each one has done.

Isaiah 48:10—Behold, I have refined you, but not as silver; I have tried you in the furnace of affliction.

Romans 8:29—For those whom he foreknew he also predestined to be conformed to the image of his Son, in order that he might be the firstborn among many brothers.

1 Peter 4:12–19—Beloved, do not be surprised at the fiery trial when it comes upon you to test you, as though something strange were happening to you. 13 But rejoice insofar as you share Christ's sufferings, that you may also rejoice and be glad when his glory is revealed. 14 If you are insulted for the name of Christ, you are blessed, because the Spirit of glory and of God rests upon you. 15 But let none of you suffer as a murderer or a thief or an evildoer or as a meddler. 16 Yet if anyone suffers as a Christian, let him not be ashamed, but let him glorify God in that name.

17 For it is time for judgment to begin at the household of God; and if it begins with us, what will be the outcome for those who do not obey the gospel of God? 18 And "If the righteous is scarcely saved, what will become of the ungodly and the sinner?" Therefore let those who suffer according to God's will entrust their souls to a faithful Creator while doing good.

Ephesians 2:8–9—For by grace you have been saved through faith. And this is not your own doing; it is the gift of God, 9 not a result of works, so that no one may boast.

Galatians 5:22–23—But the fruit of the Spirit is love, joy, peace, patience, kindness, goodness, faithfulness, 23 gentleness, self-control; against such things there is no law.

Matthew 20:28—even as the Son of Man came not to be served but to serve, and to give his life as a ransom for many."

Mark 10:45—For even the Son of Man came not to be served but to serve, and to give his life as a ransom for many."

1 Peter 1:12—It was revealed to them that they were serving not themselves but you, in the things that have now been announced to you through those who preached the good news to you by the Holy Spirit sent from heaven, things into which angels long to look.

Romans 5:3–5—Not only that, but we rejoice in our sufferings, knowing that suffering produces endurance, 4 and endurance produces character, and character produces hope, 5 and hope does not put us to shame, because God's

## TAKE HEART

love has been poured into our hearts through the Holy Spirit who has been given to us.

Romans 8:28—And we know that for those who love God all things work together for good, for those who are called according to his purpose.

2 Corinthians 1:3–7—Blessed be the God and Father of our Lord Jesus Christ, the Father of mercies and God of all comfort, 4 who comforts us in all our affliction, so that we may be able to comfort those who are in any affliction, with the comfort with which we ourselves are comforted by God. 5 For as we share abundantly in Christ's sufferings, so through Christ we share abundantly in comfort too. 6 If we are afflicted, it is for your comfort and salvation; and if we are comforted, it is for your comfort, which you experience when you patiently endure the same sufferings that we suffer. 7 Our hope for you is unshaken, for we know that as you share in our sufferings, you will also share in our comfort.

Matthew 5:4—"Blessed are those who mourn, for they shall be comforted.

James 1

Romans 8:29—For those whom he foreknew he also predestined to be conformed to the image of his Son, in order that he might be the firstborn among many brothers.

Romans 8:26–27—Likewise the Spirit helps us in our weakness. For we do not know what to pray for as we ought, but the Spirit himself intercedes for us with groanings too deep for words. 27 And he who searches hearts knows what is the mind of the Spirit, because the Spirit intercedes for the saints according to the will of God.

James 1:2—Count it all joy, my brothers, when you meet trials of various kinds,

Romans 8:28—And we know that for those who love God all things work together for good, for those who are called according to his purpose.

Matthew 16:26—For what will it profit a man if he gains the whole world and forfeits his soul? Or what shall a man give in return for his soul?

John 1:10—He was in the world, and the world was made through him, yet the world did not know him.

John 17

Colossians 2:8—See to it that no one takes you captive by philosophy and empty deceit, according to human tradition, according to the elemental spirits of the world, and not according to Christ.

Romans 11:26—And in this way all Israel will be saved, as it is written, "The Deliverer will come from Zion, he will banish ungodliness from Jacob";

Galatians 6:16—And as for all who walk by this rule, peace and mercy be upon them, and upon the Israel of God.

Exodus 16

John 6:43, 61—Jesus answered them, "Do not grumble among yourselves. But Jesus, knowing in himself that his disciples were grumbling about this, said to them, "Do you take offense at this?"

1 Peter 4:9—Show hospitality to one another without grumbling.

John 17:16—They are not of the world, just as I am not of the world.

Philippians 3:20—But our citizenship is in heaven, and from it we await a Savior, the Lord Jesus Christ,

Job 16:16—My face is red with weeping, and on my eyelids is deep darkness,

Job 19: 3–5—These ten times you have cast reproach upon me; are you not ashamed to wrong me? And even if it be true that I have erred, my error remains with myself. If indeed you magnify yourselves against me and make my disgrace an argument against me…

Job 40:4–5—Behold, I am of small account; what shall I answer you? I lay my hand on my mouth. I have spoken once, and I will not answer; twice, but I will proceed no further."

Job 42

Hebrews 3:7—Therefore, as the Holy Spirit says, "Today, if you hear his voice, do not harden your heart.

Hebrews 3:15—As it is said, "Today, if you hear his voice, do not harden your hearts as in the rebellion."

Philippians 2:1–11—So if there is any encouragement in Christ, any comfort from love, any participation in the

## JOHN O. DOZIER, JR.

Spirit, any affection and sympathy, 2 complete my joy by being of the same mind, having the same love, being in full accord and of one mind. 3 Do nothing from selfish ambition or conceit, but in humility count others more significant than yourselves. 4 Let each of you look not only to his own interests, but also to the interests of others. 5 Have this mind among yourselves, which is yours in Christ Jesus, 6 who, though he was in the form of God, did not count equality with God a thing to be grasped, 7 but emptied himself, by taking the form of a servant being born in the likeness of men. 8 And being found in human form, he humbled himself by becoming obedient to the point of death, even death on a cross. 9 Therefore God has highly exalted him and bestowed on him the name that is above every name, 10 so that at the name of Jesus every knee should bow, in heaven and on earth and under the earth, 11 and every tongue confess that Jesus Christ is Lord, to the glory of God the Father.

Galatians 5:16–26—But I say, walk by the Spirit, and you will not gratify the desires of the flesh. 17 For the desires of the flesh are against the Spirit, and the desires of the Spirit are against the flesh, for these are opposed to each other, to keep you from doing the things you want to do. 18 But if you are led by the Spirit, you are not under the law. 19 Now the works of the flesh are evident: sexual immorality, impurity, sensuality, 20 idolatry, sorcery, enmity, strife, jealousy, fits of anger, rivalries, dissensions, divisions, 21 envy, drunkenness, orgies, and things like these. I warn you, as I warned you before, that those who do such things will not inherit the kingdom of God. 22 But the fruit of the Spirit is love, joy, peace, patience, kindness, goodness, faithfulness, 23 gentleness, self-control; against such things there is no law. 24 And those who belong to Christ Jesus have crucified the flesh with its passions and desires.

Colossians 3:1–25—If then you have been raised with Christ, seek the things that are above, where Christ is, seated at the right hand of God. 2 Set your minds on things that are above, not on things that are on earth. 3 For you have died, and your life is hidden with Christ in God. 4 When Christ who is your life appears, then you also will appear with him in glory.

5 Put to death therefore what is earthly in you: sexual immorality, impurity, passion, evil desire, and covetousness, which is idolatry. 6 On account of these the wrath of God is coming. 7 In these you too once walked, when you were living in them. 8 But now you must put them all away: anger, wrath, malice, slander, and obscene talk from your mouth. 9 Do not lie to one another, seeing that you have put off the old self with its practices 10 and have put on the new self, which is being renewed in knowledge after the image of its creator. 11 Here there is not Greek and Jew, circumcised and uncircumcised, barbarian, Scythian, slave, free; but Christ is all, and in all.

12 Put on then, as God's chosen ones, holy and beloved, compassionate hearts, kindness, humility, meekness, and patience, 13 bearing with one another and, if one has a complaint against another, forgiving each other; as the Lord has forgiven you, so you also must forgive. 14 And above all these put on love, which binds everything

together in perfect harmony. 15 And let the peace of Christ rule in your hearts, to which indeed you were called in one body. And be thankful. 16 Let the word of Christ dwell in you richly, teaching and admonishing one another in all wisdom, singing psalms and hymns and spiritual songs, with thankfulness in your hearts to God. 17 And whatever you do, in word or deed, do everything in the name of the Lord Jesus, giving thanks to God the Father through him.

18 Wives, submit to your husbands, as is fitting in the Lord. 19 Husbands, love your wives, and do not be harsh with them. 20 Children, obey your parents in everything, for this pleases the Lord. 21 Fathers, do not provoke your children, lest they become discouraged. 22 Bondservants, obey in everything those who are your earthly masters, not by way of eye-service, as people-pleasers, but with sincerity of heart, fearing the Lord. 23 Whatever you do, work heartily, as for the Lord and not for men, 24 knowing that from the Lord you will receive the inheritance as your reward. You are serving the Lord Christ. 25 For the wrongdoer will be paid back for the wrong he has done, and there is no partiality.

1 John 2:6—whoever says he abides in him ought to walk in the same way in which he walked.

## In Closing: Take Close and Careful Stock of Your Heart

1 Chronicles 16:15—Remember his covenant forever, the word that he commanded, for a thousand generations,

## TAKE HEART

Psalm 111:5—He provides food for those who fear him; he remembers his covenant forever.

Jeremiah 31:33–34—For this is the covenant that I will make with the house of Israel after those days, declares the LORD: I will put my law within them, and I will write it on their hearts. And I will be their God, and they shall be my people. 34 And no longer shall each one teach his neighbor and each his brother, saying, 'Know the LORD,' for they shall all know me, from the least of them to the greatest, declares the LORD. For I will forgive their iniquity, and I will remember their sin no more."

1 Corinthians 15:1–3—Now I would remind you, brothers, of the gospel I preached to you, which you received, in which you stand, 2 and by which you are being saved, if you hold fast to the word I preached to you—unless you believed in vain. For I delivered to you as of first importance what I also received: that Christ died for our sins in accordance with the Scriptures…

2 Timothy 1:6—For this reason I remind you to fan into flame the gift of God, which is in you through the laying on of my hands,

2 Timothy 2:8—Remember Jesus Christ, risen from the dead, the offspring of David, as preached in my gospel,

2 Peter 1:12–21—Therefore I intend always to remind you of these qualities, though you know them and are established in the truth that you have. 13 I think it right, as long as I am in this body, to stir you up by way of reminder, 14 since I know that the putting off of my body will be

soon, as our Lord Jesus Christ made clear to me. 15 And I will make every effort so that after my departure you may be able at any time to recall these things.

16 For we did not follow cleverly devised myths when we made known to you the power and coming of our Lord Jesus Christ, but we were eyewitnesses of his majesty. 17 For when he received honor and glory from God the Father, and the voice was borne to him by the Majestic Glory, "This is my beloved Son, with whom I am well pleased," 18 we ourselves heard this very voice borne from heaven, for we were with him on the holy mountain. 19 And we have the prophetic word more fully confirmed, to which you will do well to pay attention as to a lamp shining in a dark place, until the day dawns and the morning star rises in your hearts, 20 knowing this first of all, that no prophecy of Scripture comes from someone's own interpretation. 21 For no prophecy was ever produced by the will of man, but men spoke from God as they were carried along by the Holy Spirit.

Ephesians 4:15—Rather, speaking the truth in love, we are to grow up in every way into him who is the head, into Christ.

James 1:2–4—Count it all joy, my brothers, when you meet trials of various kinds, 3 for you know that the testing of your faith produces steadfastness. 4 And let steadfastness have its full effect, that you may be perfect and complete, lacking in nothing.

1 Peter 5:10—And after you have suffered a little while, the God of all grace, who has called you to his eternal glory

in Christ, will himself restore, confirm, strengthen, and establish you.

Romans 5:3–5—Not only that, but we rejoice in our sufferings, knowing that suffering produces endurance, 4 and endurance produces character, and character produces hope, 5 and hope does not put us to shame, because God's love has been poured into our hearts through the Holy Spirit who has been given to us.

1 Thessalonians 5:23—Now may the God of peace himself sanctify you completely, and may your whole spirit and soul and body be kept blameless at the coming of our Lord Jesus Christ.

2 Timothy 2:21—Therefore, if anyone cleanses himself from what is dishonorable, he will be a vessel for honorable use, set apart as holy, useful to the master of the house, ready for every good work.

Psalm 126:5—Those who sow in tears shall reap with shouts of joy!

2 Corinthians 1:3–7—Blessed be the God and Father of our Lord Jesus Christ, the Father of mercies and God of all comfort, 4 who comforts us in all our affliction, so that we may be able to comfort those who are in any affliction, with the comfort with which we ourselves are comforted by God. 5 For as we share abundantly in Christ's sufferings, so through Christ we share abundantly in comfort too. 6 If we are afflicted, it is for your comfort and salvation; and if we are comforted, it is for your comfort, which you experience when you patiently endure the same

sufferings that we suffer. 7 Our hope for you is unshaken, for we know that as you share in our sufferings, you will also share in our comfort.

1 Peter 5:1–5—So I exhort the elders among you, as a fellow elder and a witness of the sufferings of Christ, as well as a partaker in the glory that is going to be revealed: 2 shepherd the flock of God that is among you, exercising oversight not under compulsion, but willingly, as God would have you; not for shameful gain, but eagerly; 3 not domineering over those in your charge, but being examples to the flock. 4 And when the chief Shepherd appears, you will receive the unfading crown of glory. 5 Likewise, you who are younger, be subject to the elders. Clothe yourselves, all of you, with humility toward one another, for "God opposes the proud but gives grace to the humble."

1 Timothy 3:1–7—The saying is trustworthy: If anyone aspires to the office of overseer, he desires a noble task. 2 Therefore an overseer must be above reproach, the husband of one wife, sober-minded, self-controlled, respectable, hospitable, able to teach, 3 not a drunkard, not violent but gentle, not quarrelsome, not a lover of money. 4 He must manage his own household well, with all dignity keeping his children submissive, 5 for if someone does not know how to manage his own household, how will he care for God's church? 6 He must not be a recent convert, or he may become puffed up with conceit and fall into the condemnation of the devil. 7 Moreover, he must be well thought of by outsiders, so that he may not fall into disgrace, into a snare of the devil.

## TAKE HEART

Romans 8:18—For I consider that the sufferings of this present time are not worth comparing with the glory that is to be revealed to us.

1 Peter 4:12–19—Beloved, do not be surprised at the fiery trial when it comes upon you to test you, as though something strange were happening to you. 13 But rejoice insofar as you share Christ's sufferings, that you may also rejoice and be glad when his glory is revealed. 14 If you are insulted for the name of Christ, you are blessed, because the Spirit of glory and of God rests upon you. 15 But let none of you suffer as a murderer or a thief or an evildoer or as a meddler. 16 Yet if anyone suffers as a Christian, let him not be ashamed, but let him glorify God in that name. 17 For it is time for judgment to begin at the household of God; and if it begins with us, what will be the outcome for those who do not obey the gospel of God? 18 And, "If the righteous is scarcely saved, what will become of the ungodly and the sinner?" Therefore let those who suffer according to God's will entrust their souls to a faithful Creator while doing good.

1 John 1:9—If we confess our sins, he is faithful and just to forgive us our sins and to cleanse us from all unrighteousness.

1 Corinthians 6:9–10—Or do you not know that the unrighteous will not inherit the kingdom of God? Do not be deceived: neither the sexually immoral, nor idolaters, nor adulterers, nor men who practice homosexuality, 10 nor thieves, nor the greedy, nor drunkards, nor revilers, nor swindlers will inherit the kingdom of God.

Ezekiel 11:17–21—Therefore say, 'Thus says the Lord GOD: I will gather you from the peoples and assemble you out of the countries where you have been scattered, and I will give you the land of Israel.' 18 And when they come there, they will remove from it all its detestable things and all its abominations. 19 And I will give them one heart, and a new spirit I will put within them. I will remove the heart of stone from their flesh and give them a heart of flesh, 20 that they may walk in my statutes and keep my rules and obey them. And they shall be my people, and I will be their God. 21 But as for those whose heart goes after their detestable things and their abominations, I will bring their deeds upon their own heads, declares the Lord GOD."

Ezekiel 36:26—And I will give you a new heart, and a new spirit I will put within you. And I will remove the heart of stone from your flesh and give you a heart of flesh.

John 17:21—that they may all be one, just as you, Father, are in me, and I in you, that they also may be in us, so that the world may believe that you have sent me.

1 Peter 5:8—Be sober-minded; be watchful. Your adversary the devil prowls around like a roaring lion, seeking someone to devour.

John 14:16—And I will ask the Father, and he will give you another Helper, to be with you forever,

John 14:26—But the Helper, the Holy Spirit, whom the Father will send in my name, he will teach you all things and bring to your remembrance all that I have said to you.

## TAKE HEART

2 Corinthians 1:22—and who has also put his seal on us and given us his Spirit in our hearts as a guarantee...

Matthew 28:16–20—Now the eleven disciples went to Galilee, to the mountain to which Jesus had directed them. 17 And when they saw him they worshiped him, but some doubted. 18 And Jesus came and said to them, "All authority in heaven and on earth has been given to me. 19 Go therefore and make disciples of all nations, baptizing them in[a] the name of the Father and of the Son and of the Holy Spirit, 20 teaching them to observe all that I have commanded you. And behold, I am with you always, to the end of the age."

1 Thessalonians 2:19–20—For what is our hope or joy or crown of boasting before our Lord Jesus at his coming? Is it not you? For you are our glory and joy.

1 John 2:15–17—Do not love the world or the things in the world. If anyone loves the world, the love of the Father is not in him. 16 For all that is in the world—the desires of the flesh and the desires of the eyes and pride of life[a]—is not from the Father but is from the world. 17 And the world is passing away along with its desires, but whoever does the will of God abides forever.

Romans 12:2—Do not be conformed to this world,[a] but be transformed by the renewal of your mind, that by testing you may discern what is the will of God, what is good and acceptable and perfect.

Colossians 3:2—Set your minds on things that are above, not on things that are on earth.

Romans 8:8—Those who are in the flesh cannot please God.

1 Corinthians 6:18—Flee from sexual immorality. Every other sin a person commits is outside the body, but the sexually immoral person sins against his own body.

Galatians 5:17—For the desires of the flesh are against the Spirit, and the desires of the Spirit are against the flesh, for these are opposed to each other, to keep you from doing the things you want to do.

1 Peter 5:8—Be sober-minded; be watchful. Your adversary the devil prowls around like a roaring lion, seeking someone to devour.

James 4:7—Submit yourselves therefore to God. Resist the devil, and he will flee from you.

Ephesians 6:11–12—Put on the whole armor of God, that you may be able to stand against the schemes of the devil. 12 For we do not wrestle against flesh and blood, but against the rulers, against the authorities, against the cosmic powers over this present darkness, against the spiritual forces of evil in the heavenly places.

John 8:44—You are of your father the devil, and your will is to do your father's desires. He was a murderer from the beginning, and does not stand in the truth, because there is no truth in him. When he lies, he speaks out of his own character, for he is a liar and the father of lies.

2 Corinthians 1:3–5—Blessed be the God and Father of our Lord Jesus Christ, the Father of mercies and God of

all comfort, 4 who comforts us in all our affliction, so that we may be able to comfort those who are in any affliction, with the comfort with which we ourselves are comforted by God. 5 For as we share abundantly in Christ's sufferings, so through Christ we share abundantly in comfort too.

Philippians 2:1–11—(Conformed to Christ.) So if there is any encouragement in Christ, any comfort from love, any participation in the Spirit, any affection and sympathy, 2 complete my joy by being of the same mind, having the same love, being in full accord and of one mind. 3 Do nothing from selfish ambition or conceit, but in humility count others more significant than yourselves. 4 Let each of you look not only to his own interests, but also to the interests of others. 5 Have this mind among yourselves, which is yours in Christ Jesus, 6 who, though he was in the form of God, did not count equality with God a thing to be grasped, 7 but emptied himself, by taking the form of a servant, being born in the likeness of men. 8 And being found in human form, he humbled himself by becoming obedient to the point of death, even death on a cross. 9 Therefore God has highly exalted him and bestowed on him the name that is above every name, 10 so that at the name of Jesus every knee should bow, in heaven and on earth and under the earth, 11 and every tongue confess that Jesus Christ is Lord, to the glory of God the Father.

1 Corinthians 4:5—Therefore do not pronounce judgment before the time, before the Lord comes, who will bring to light the things now hidden in darkness and will disclose

the purposes of the heart. Then each one will receive his commendation from God.

2 Corinthians 5:10—For we must all appear before the judgment seat of Christ, so that each one may receive what is due for what he has done in the body, whether good or evil.

# God's Redemptive Plan

## Take Heart!
## There's a Person, a Promise, and Perfect Plan in Place

One of my favorite passages of the Bible is a simple, yet supremely important promise, "For God is not the author of confusion but of peace, as in all the churches of the saints" (1 Corinthians 14:33, KJV). No, the God of the Bible is not a God of chaos or disarray he is the God of order. His plan for our salvation creates peace within our heart our spirit and our life. Do you want God's person, peace, purpose, and plan in your heart?

A variety of issues at work in our culture, our churches, and our own hearts today can give the impression that the people of God are as uncertain and confused as the world around us about the Bible, the God who inspired it, and his redemptive plan. Sometimes, this uncertainty and confusion tempts the church to entertain substitute theologies or to flail in antagonism at those who espouse the True Truth of the Bible.

Uncertainty and confusion, along with their first cousins, worry and anxiety, are killers of the human heart. God created us in his image, to love him with all our heart, mind, soul, and strength. Our hearts were not made for confusion. Please, beloved, don't blame God for the confusion and uncertainty his people sometimes express.

And don't let it stir up doubts in your heart concerning his plan for your salvation. God has made nothing truly important to be a mystery to us. He does not intend to confuse you.

The fact is, God loves the world and has devised a very specific plan for it—the Plan of Redemption. How illogical would it be for the one who so carefully created you, the one who made you the culmination, the pinnacle of his creation, to leave you twisting in the wind, confused and despairing, over issues of eternal life and death!

No, God has displayed the truth about his awesome person, plan, story, and glory in what he has done to rescue us, his beloved image-bearers, from the misery, pain, shame, and fear that befell us when we fell into sin. Human beings have long tried to resolve this problem by creating religions and schemes by which we reached out to God, presenting to him supposed "good works" by which to merit his favor. These efforts never provided more than momentary, hollow relief. And they resulted in only hearts more hardened still. Pursuing peace with God by any means other than the means of redemption he himself has provided always results in hardening. Only God's plan of redemption creates the Shalom our hearts most deeply desire. Only that plan demonstrates for you and for the world God's deep delight in you!

The Good News is that the God of the Bible has done everything necessary to secure for us peace with him and within us. He offers it freely to us as a gift—a free gift of God's grace, a gift that cost God the life of his one only

## *TAKE HEART*

Son. God expects us to receive that gift with realistic self-awareness, brokenness, relief, joy, and a deep gratitude that bears the fruit of righteousness and devotion. Please don't cheapen that gift by proposing to add your own merit to it. Rather, just receive it! Receive it as the free gift God intended it to be.

To help you unpack that gift with deeper appreciation and hope, I have included here an explanation of various key facets. A few pages cannot begin to exhaust the beauty of the plan. Nor can it hope to delve deeply into all the details. But it does explain that plan in broad and biblical strokes. While my words are fallible, the plan itself cannot fail! It is built on the character and promises of God.

Read on to discover the unsurpassed joy of knowing more deeply the infinite, yet intimate God who is at work in you and for you, the God who wants you to receive the spectacular benefits of his redeeming work.

1. Effectual Calling—This is the supernatural work of God's Holy Spirit, by his own sovereign and free will, to convince a person of his sin and misery, enlighten his mind in the knowledge of Christ, and renew, persuade, and enable him to embrace Christ as he is freely offered in the gospel. "This effectual call is of God's free and special grace alone, not from anything at all foreseen in man, who is altogether passive therein, until, being quickened and renewed by the Holy Spirit, he is thereby enabled to answer

this call, and to embrace the grace offered and conveyed in it.[i]

2. Regeneration—This work of God is closely, yet mysteriously, linked with his effectual calling so that the two could conceivably be considered one simultaneous work of God. It is distinguished as that act of God's grace whereby he supernaturally implants a new, Christ-aware heart and spiritual life in us so that our internal spiritual governance changes. It "carries with it the operative grace whereby a person called is enabled to answer [God's specific and effectual] call...to embrace Jesus Christ as he is freely offered in the gospel."[ii] This supernatural work of the Triune God working separately and in union is frequently illustrated in Scripture as God's gift of a new heart, a heart that is alive and honorably responsive to Biblical truth. It is God's work alone that initially changes the heart, and yet Christians are called to evangelize and make disciples. This apparent contradiction or tension is God's to command and ours to obey, nonetheless.[iii]

3. Faith and Repentance—These actions are demonstrated only by those whom God has first effectually called and regenerated. They are interdependent so that faith leads to repentance and repentance requires true faith. Faith,

---

[i] Westminster Confession of Faith; see also Matthew 22:14; John 6:37; Romans 8:7-9; 30; 9:11; 1 Corinthians 1:9; Ephesians 2:8-9; 2 Timothy 1:9; and 1 John 3:1; 3:9; 5:1.
[ii] Berkhoff, Systematic Theology
[iii] See Ezekiel 11:19; 36:26-26; John 1:13; 3:8; 6:44-45; 1 Corinthians 2:5,12, 14; 2 Corinthians 3:3, 6; 1 John 2:29, 3:9, 4:7, 5:1, 4, 18; James 1:18; and 2 Thessalonians 2:13-14.

therefore, consists of knowledge, conviction and trust specifically in Christ as Lord and Savior as he is presented in the gospel.[iv] Repentance, most simply, means "to turn." Christian repentance is a specific kind of turning. It happens when we are first made aware of and grieved by our sin and our utter confusion apart from Jesus Christ as Savior and Lord. We then hate the sin and turn away from it to Christ for mercy, forgiveness, and the grace for new obedience—all based upon gratitude and no longer hoping to earn merit of any kind for ourselves.[v]

4. Justification—How can sinful people be just or right with a holy God, and therefore justified before our Judge? This also is a work of God alone and is a gift from him, a gift freely offered to those whom he effectually calls and regenerates. It has to do with how we are made just (legally right, righteous, or "at peace") with the God of the Bible. More specifically, justification is an act of God's free grace which takes place at one specific point in time. It involves his freely pardoning all our sins and declaring us righteous, not based on anything we have done, but solely upon the righteous life and sin-paying death of Jesus Christ.[vi]

5. Adoption—"But as many as received him, to them gave he the authority to become children of God, to those who

---

[iv] See Isaiah 45:21-22; Ezekiel 33:11, 18:23, 32; Romans 19:17; and Ephesians 2:8.

[v] See Thessalonians 1:9-10; Luke 24:46-47; Acts 2:37-38, 5:3; Romans 6:2, 6; and Hebrews 6:1.

[vi] See Deuteronomy 25:1; Psalm 89:15-16; Proverbs 17:15; Romans 3:14, 20, 4:2, 10:3, 8:33-34; Galatians 2:16, 3:11, 5:4; and Philippians 3:9.

believe in his name" (John 1:12). We become children of God because he bestows that right upon us. He gives this right to all who believe on Jesus' name. God adopts believers in Christ, and we become his own children. This adoption is the embrace of God made possible by justification. In this joyous movement of God, he receives those he has justified as his own children, puts his name upon them, gives his Spirit to them, and binds them to himself forever for his care and protection.[vii]

6. Sanctification—This is a continual work of God's grace that begins at justification and ends at glorification. As the word implies, sanctification involves God's "scrubbing program," carried out by him as he graciously and sovereignly applies the realities of the Gospel and the various Christian disciplines to the hearts of his regenerated, justified, adopted, and faithful people. In so doing, God works to release us from the power of sin and grows us up to be more like Christ, both in our inward thoughts and outward behaviors. In regeneration, God gives us new hearts. In sanctification, he nourishes and strengthens that new heart, sheltering it so that it may grow as a tender vine to full, fruit-bearing Christian maturity.

Christians are called to be willing participants with God in this grand work of sanctification, much like a little child is called to cooperate with his mom who is giving him a bath. Cooperation does not necessarily or ultimately determine whether growth happens. But it does certainly determine

---

[vii] See Matthew 6:9; Romans 8:15-16; 1 Corinthians 2: 9-10, and Galatians 4:6.

the joy and depth of the endeavor to the one sanctified. True Truth, as it has its way in the re-born human heart, sanctifies it. In contrast, when falsehood has its way, it condemns, defiles, desecrates, and disintegrates our hearts.

Ultimately, we are sanctified and made more holy, not for ourselves, but for service. Sanctification sets us apart for serving God by serving those around us—just as Jesus came, not to be served, but to serve. We grow more and more like him as God applies the Gospel to our lives, day by day.[viii]

7. Perseverance—Like all that has come before, perseverance has to do with God's work in and for his adopted children. Many mistakenly pivot perseverance on a new Christian's dutiful discipline or continued faithfulness. While these things are essential to our experience of security in Christ, they do not determine it. Perseverance is a work of God whereby he seals and secures his adopted children as such to the very end, to glorification. This Christian teaching glorifies God in his kingly power to keep his children spiritually safe in his arms for all time. It is upon this platform of divine security that an adopted child of God joyfully, not fearfully, nourishes his relationship with Christ and freely, not full of guilt, serves him.

---

[viii] See Matthew 5:48; Romans 7:22; 1 Corinthians 2:14-15; 1 Corinthians 15:54; Phil 3:21; 1 John 2:16, 3:3, 4:4, Deuteronomy 30:1-10; John 14; and the Book of Titus.

The lesson of the seed sowed on rocky ground,[ix] is that the seed took root and sprang up, but when the sun rose, it was scorched (the heat of the battle) and brought forth no fruit. It did not persevere. Jesus said, "If you abide in my word, you are truly my disciples, and you will know the truth, and the truth will set you free" (John 8:31-32). Everyone who is truly called is called to persevere. As Paul wrote, "Not that I have already obtained this or am already perfect, but I press on to make it my own, because Christ Jesus has made me his own. Brothers, I do not consider that I have made it my own. But one thing I do: forgetting what lies behind and straining forward to what lies ahead, I press on toward the goal for the prize of the upward call of God in Christ Jesus" (Philippians 3:12-14).

8. Glorification—If justification is God's freeing his people from the penalty of sin, and sanctification is his freeing us from the power of sin, then glorification is his freeing us completely from the presence of sin. Even more, glorification is God's giving us, his beloved, adopted children, other indescribable gifts as well:

•Impenetrably holy souls.

•Unfettered and direct access to himself.

•Complete freedom from all sin and misery, and pure and unending pleasures of immeasurable magnitude.

Like justification, this is an instantaneous change that will take place for the whole company of the redeemed in

---

[ix] See Mark 4: 5-6, 16-17

Christ when Christ will come again in glory to judge the living and the dead. He will descend from heaven with a shout as he triumphs over death, the last enemy:

*Then we'll come to pass this chain that is written, death is swallowed up in victory. Oh death, where is thy victory? Oh death, where is thy sting?"*
*(1 Corinthians 15:54-55).*

*"Rejoice", Peter writes, "insofar as you share Christ's sufferings, that you may also rejoice and be glad when his glory is revealed"*
*(1 Peter 4:13)*

Glorification has cosmic proportions:

*According to his promise we are waiting for new heavens and a new earth in which righteousness dwells*
*(2 Peter 3:13).*

*Then comes the end, when he delivers the kingdom to God the Father after destroying every rule and every authority and power*
*(1 Corinthians 15:24).*

*JOHN O. DOZIER, JR.*

# Union with Jesus Christ:
# The Context for all God's Work

If anything is clear from the plan of redemption described here, it is that God alone is the Initiator and actor. He either does the work directly (as in justification), or he makes that work possible (as in faith and repentance). While we have a duty to respond to his actions, what should be equally clear of is the absolutely astounding fact that God gives us a new heart and everything that flows from it as free gifts and expects us to receive them with joy and gratitude. He gives them despite the fact that we are so undeserving. In fact, we deserve precisely the opposite!

Still, you may be asking, "Since I am so undeserving, how is it that God offers me these gifts?" Good question! He offers them to you based on something called "union with Christ." In brief, this is a phrase the Bible uses more than 160 times to describe God's working an "intimate, vital, and spiritual joining together of Christ and his people, in virtue of which he is the source of their life and strength, of their blessedness and salvation."[x] Adopted children of God receive his blessings because Jesus deserved God's blessings. Since God put us in Jesus, we get to enjoy God's blessings, too!

For example, in Jesus by faith, we died with him on Calvary's cross. In Jesus by faith, we rose with Christ when God raised him from the dead. Similarly, all the other blessings that come along with the new birth belong to us,

---

[x] Berkhoff, Systematic Theology

all because the Father has placed us in Christ. Celebrate these astounding provisions of God today![xi]

Union with Christ is the central truth in the whole doctrine of salvation. All to which the people of God have been predestined in the eternal election of God, all that has been secured and procured for them in the once and for all accomplishment of redemption, all of which they become the actual partakers in the application of redemption, and all that by God's grace they will become in the state of glorification is embraced within the compass of union and communion with Christ. Not only does the new life of regeneration faith, repentance, justification, and adoption have as its inception being in Christ, it is also continued by virtue of the same relationship to him.

For now, we live in Christ as we go about our everyday activities. It is in Christ that believers are dead to sin and that we are resurrected. When Christ returns, the union will be complete.[xii] Glorification with Christ at his second coming will mark the beginning of that consummation as Jesus makes all things new and ushers in the New Heavens and New Earth.

**Amen! And Amen.**

---

[xi] See Romans. 6:23, 8:1, 39, 1 Corinthians 1:2, 15:18, Ephesians 1-2, Colossians 1-2: and 1 Peter 5:10.

[xii] See Romans 6: 4; 1 Corinthians1:4, 5; and 1 Corinthians 6:15-17.

# About the Author

John Dozier, President of Feast of the Heart, LLC, is a men's ministry leader and spiritual mentor to many. He has been active in his church and elsewhere as a Bible-based leadership coach, organizational consultant, and Stephen's Minister.

John has a passion for encouraging others to see how God transforms tragedy into triumph and facilitating Christ-centered reformation, revival and constructive revolution. His professional experience spans for-profit and non-profit organizations in the areas of leadership coaching, organizational effectiveness, strategic planning, marketing, advertising, purchasing, merchandising, branding, public relations and communications.

John and his wife, Peggy, currently reside in St. Louis, Missouri. They have two married children, Polly [Will], and Teddy [Allison] and three grandchildren, Ellery, Rebecca and Laurel.

**Contact:**

**www.feastoftheheart.org**

# About
# Feast of the Heart, LLC:

Focused on helping bring about "Reformation, Revival, Constructive Revolution" (Francis Schaeffer) to fruition by:

- Publishing—"The Weeping, The Window, The Way" (on suffering), Facebook, Blogs
- Training Table—A weekly e-mail diet for running the good race.
- Speaking Engagements
- Book Signings, Conferences, Seminars, "Brown Bags"
- Spiritual Coaching—Serve as a listener, sounding board, and catalyst for spiritual "reformation, revival, constructive revolution" maturity.
- Fellowship, Feast of the Heart Adventure Retreats—Wednesday thru Sunday (or longer) outdoor, wilderness retreats that combine physical exertion, groveling in nature, along with spiritual growth in the fellowship of like-hearted people.

**Contact:**

**www.feastoftheheart.org**